SWEET
ENVY

Sweet Envy

SWEET ENVY

ALISTAIR WISE &
TEENA KEARNEY-WISE

MURDOCH BOOKS

CONTENTS

FROM HERE TO THERE

OUR LITTLE CAKE SHOP in Hobart has history. Before it was a travel agent and vegie shop, it was the Gem cake shop, and the oldies still regale us with their tales of Neenish tarts and queen cakes.

The biggest question we are asked is why did we leave New York — the Big Apple — for Tasmania, the Little Apple? It's simple: here, we could afford to set up, and with a bit of work we can get hold of *amazing* seasonal produce: morello cherries, figs, mulberries, greengage plums, banana passionfruit and even artichokes, just to name a few... Right down to the dairy goods from the north of the state, we get a fantastic array of seasonal produce through backdoor deals and shopside barters. You'd have to be an idiot to not embrace your local people, and share or barter some produce. The days of 'locavore' are over: it is mandatory, not exceptional. Local produce tastes better and is often cheaper.

Our shop is more than a way of generating an income: it's our home. Our beautiful daughter Matilda cannot remember life outside the cake shop. She has learnt to walk here, and honed her social skills by bouncing from table to table chatting with customers.

There is no tsunami-wave of punters flowing into our shop: we are off the main tourist strip. We don't stick to some formulated plan, we make whatever we are into at the moment. We are a small team, we make it fresh, and if we run out, we shut shop early. There's a savoury selection for the regulars, and sometimes I need a sausage roll for lunch too. We make bread on the weekends, as we love toast on our days off. We have added Big Bessie, our ice-cream truck, as our massive expansion. And that's about it.

Most of all, we do not take ourselves too seriously. We are just a simple neighbourhood cake shop. Not a patisserie, because that would make us way too proper, and not a bakery, as we don't bake enough bread — probably more a diner-cum-greasy spoon that sells cake. We are somewhere you can take the kids and hang out, or slip by for a few sweeties. If it's for an event, chat with Teena and she will whip you up a special cake into any form you can imagine.

IN THE BEGINNING...

Teena and I are from families that cook a lot, although reading cookbooks these days, it would now seem essential that a passion for food runs through your veins.

We both started in the same little pastry shop in Hobart, La Cuisine, which is where we met. It was one of the first, and established its reputation long before Hobart turned into a bakery town in which bakers now outnumber the old 'chippers' two to one. The curtain that hung over the upstairs window had a poorly drawn coffee cup on it and was stained from a leaky roof, all the stock was kept upstairs on the narrow, carpeted flour-trodden steps, but it was a good place for a little canoodling.

We competed in pastry competitions as a way to break the monotony: like most youngsters, we felt the grass was always greener somewhere else and we saw it as a way to escape. Young and naive, huh.

I was lucky enough to win a spot on the Australian team for an international leg in Montreal. On the last day of the competition, the judges from all the countries were

muttering a few pooh-poohs in my direction, as my attempts at creating fine pastry had not all been too successful. Today was wedding cake day, but somehow I had missed the memo or it had been lost in translation. Most other entrants had spent months training on a single dish and all I had to work with was a few scrappy palette knives. At this point winning was not an option, so I figured if you cannot be famous, be notorious. The judges stared in disbelief as I stuck a dunny (an Aussie outback toilet) on top of my cake, complete with a redback spider, then inscribed country singer Slim Dusty's 'bush psalm' upon the cake. The French and Italian judges reeled in horror, but holy mother of god, the last day was the best.

Teena came second in the pastry-making nationals, but because the guy who won was over the age limit for the international round, she won the spot to represent Australia in Seoul. Teena, a much better strategist than I, came in the top ten.

OFF TO THE BIG ISLAND

After exhausting the Hobart scene, it was time to hit the 'big island', as Tasmanians call the Australian mainland. I took off to Melbourne; Teena followed six months later. It was a hectic time of bouncing around the traps, but after living through a few wine-cellar tantrums and restaurants closing overnight with ill-tempered Frenchmen, I ended up as pastry chef at Circa the Prince, in the Michael Lambie era, while Teena ran the pastry department at The Point restaurant in Albert Park, under the watchful gaze of Ian Curley, his arms full of tattoos as he sipped nothing but champagne.

Circa was amazing. The band room and the Van Handel brothers' wide sphere of influence saw a never-ending stream of brilliant after-parties that we'd slip through the back door to see — although Prince sipping red wine from a glass with a straw seemed less rock 'n' roll than we would have liked. We took any excuse to pretend to check bookings so we could slip by and see a celebrity. Legendary chef David Thompson came to Circa and cooked an exclusive dinner: nobody cooks with that deftness of touch with a Cosmopolitan in their hand. Those days were ridiculously fun, yet slightly taxing, as Melbourne was in the grip of an almost *Wolf of Wall Street* substance-abuse problem.

Teena had some great events at The Point. Situated in the middle of Albert Park, the restaurant is home to the 'who's who' of racing for the Grand Prix, so she'd get to trundle in during this spectacular event to watch the fine beasts tearing up the tarmac. Immersed in the adrenalin of racing, she was pulled up more than once for attempting a race time in our Suzuki Sierra soft-top on the way to work.

LONDON CALLING

Melbourne done, it was time to move on. We packed a backpack and landed at Heathrow with no real plan. Take it as it comes, go with the flow... what the hell were we thinking!

Chancing our arm, we phoned around at the airport before catching the train into London. I rang Gordon Ramsay's head office and got a trial with chef patron Angela Hartnett at the Connaught hotel, while Teena tried to find us somewhere to live, as we'd only booked a hotel for the first three nights.

Working with Angela was brilliant. She rejected most of my first attempts to get a dessert on the menu, mostly because they were too cloying, and in hindsight damn ugly. Angela taught me a new way to cook: more feminine and nurturing, and less like a man dominating ingredients. Slowly the pastry team took more on, and soon we had an afternoon tea trolley, with the wonderful bakers Arlet and Alum to do the baking... although Alum, a Muslim, sometimes fell asleep during prayer time, incinerating the *viennoiserie*, and I would trot down the stairs into billowing clouds of noxious smoke.

Teena after a while gave up her dream of working in a cake shop, as these were mostly located in outer London, and commuting for three hours each way in unknown territory

seemed a little daunting. She returned to restaurants and worked at The Greenhouse with head chef Bjorn van der Horst, who was back in London after his stint with legendary chef Alain Ducasse — although his somewhat blind optimism in letting the sous chefs wow him with what dishes should go on the *menu du jour* and trying to get squirrel recognised as the new protein of choice left us bewildered. Thierry Besselievre was the pastry chef, a stalwart hardened from battle after long tenures with the Roux brothers, the gourmet food company Fauchon, and even Gordon Ramsay; his skills were quite exceptional, but he was a little fond of matchmaking sites.

After our adventures finding bits to build a cake for the Chelsea Football Club, Teena landed a job in Putney, at Cakes 4 Fun. One of Teena's first days alone running the kitchen and shop front while the boss was on holiday was filled with turmoil, when a lovely lady came to pick up her christening cake of a three-dimensional baby... and the baby was the wrong skin colour! Luckily it was fixed within the hour to resemble the lady's beautiful bouncing baby boy.

With Teena's cake-shop hours being much better than those of restaurants (which are way too many), Teena had the chance to get us tickets to all that Europe had to offer, although everyone thought we were bonkers taking our chance to run with bulls, throw tomatoes or shoot off to Paris for a quick tub of Le Vacherin Mont D'or, a gooey washed-rind cheese.

Our first true epiphany came when French chef Joël Robuchon cooked at the Connaught. He is a small man, but the chefs in the kitchen tiptoed around him as if Elvis was in the building. I was in the office banging away on some costings, and a very quietly spoken Joël asked what I was doing. 'Costings,' I said, 'to see if I can afford to make this dish for Angela...' Mystified, he looked at me with piercing eyes, the kind of look that sucks the life from your overeager intentions, like a Potter-esque dementor. He simply stated in monotone, 'Cook the dish, make sure it tastes great, and charge what you have to.' Sage advice.

Visas up, it was time to leave London. We were back in Hobart, about to start a new life, when we got a call asking if we wanted to work in New York City.

It was a once in a lifetime moment. It wasn't the plan, but we had to go.

THE BIG APPLE BECKONS

Gordon Ramsay's hotel, The London NYC, was hellfire and brimstone. Teena and I had rebanded after years of not working together. I was executive pastry chef, while Teena had the almighty job of containing the production kitchen, as well as being the safe set of hands needed in a crisis. She kept the production kitchen running with its rag-tag motley crew, while I tried to hold the service kitchen in some kind of order. My head was still in London, where the art of screaming had been well learnt — but all that led to in this city was arbitration with a union delegate. It was time to chill out or get an ulcer.

Kitchen staff ran off with sommeliers and drank Dom Pérignon straight from the bottle with hookers in the unfinished executive suites upstairs in the 580-room hotel, as the kitchen ran into a quagmire of rehashed and out-of-date cuisine. It was pure chaos. The big dogs flew in to sort out the mess, which led to Gordon Ramsay kicking the fish and meat sections 'off the line' and cooking it himself. Electricity was in the air, the kitchen sang with billowing voices of 'Oui, chef!' and Gordon, whilst cooking, still picked me up on a water mark on a spoon at ten paces. The legends are real: this man could cook in a dizzying display of sheer prowess. Still, friends were lost and nerves frayed.

It was now summer and blistering hot. We are from Tassie, we like it cool. The sweat dripped from the nose, the tempered chocolate cylinder melted in the pastry chef's clammy grip, and Teena was on the pass, trying to help us out of a never-ending relentless Armageddon service. We'd walk home in flip-flops as rats ran over the trash heaps in the street. After one long week we trudged around the East Village and the Meatpacking District in a haze, and stumbled upon tiny shops and cafes reeking with delicious food and great banter. What these guys and girls were having was fun. No braggard chefs' jackets starched an inch from cardboard; no pristine black pants; no lunchtime rendezvous for medis and pedis or glowing orange spray tans. These guys had tatts, were having fun, and were engaged in a way we had forgotten about.

It was time to move on. Unquestionably, it was time to go home. But what to do?

It was time for our own venture.

BACK TO THE LITTLE APPLE

We had no real plan and no real budget — hell, we'd worked in kitchens all our lives, and our life savings were meagre. Back in Hobart, pastry jobs were hard to come by, so Teena started up in a florist's. I worked in a parlous, filthy little cafe that was ridden with off food: behind every bench lurked the slops of Christmas past. Dodgy dealings with the devil of a landlord and a staff member meant that business was doomed to fail.

On those long flights back to Hobart, I'd finally had time to read Anthony Bourdain's *Kitchen Confidential*. Now it was time to put one of his philosophies to the test: could I stay to the end at that squalid little cafe, and trade equipment in lieu of wages? The cafe owner and I agreed upon a bench dough sheeter, mixer, trays and a few racks for the unpaid wages: a great start, but nowhere near enough. Justin from Jackman & McRoss bakery cafe put me on and I tried to behave, but sometimes had the pleasure of stirring up big Rik, a kung fu-obsessed Maori with a temper.

Then one day, a strange little man pulled up in the car park offering his organic vegies to the kitchen, a conversation began, and he told me he was looking to get rid of a business in North Hobart. Hooked, I followed him to his shop — an organic grocer's littered with boxes in various states of decay. The bones though were beautiful, even if in federation green.

We discussed a deal as his wife sat on a stool in the littered kitchen, dipping regular bananas in red wax to make them 'organic'. Their asking price was way too high; eventually we settled for less than half his original price.

He left us with all the rotting vegetables, weeds ten feet high, a dungeon full of rats, and a landlady who had no idea that her previous tenant was moving on. A new lease signed, our families came round and looked at us as if we'd lost our minds. But it was all we could afford, and we had no idea how to get a backer. We pulled everything out of the shop and looked at the hiding holes in the floor with disbelief. Our landlord Mrs Cogan agreed to patch the floor, so we set about getting the plumbing works done and badgered Elliott, my youngest brother, who was now an electrician, into checking the electricals, although most of his advice was ignored as it would simply cost too much.

We wanted a cabinet like one we had seen at New York's Chelsea Market, so we drew on the floor with chalk and took some measurements. Teena designed the cabinet and set about getting it made, liaising with all the suppliers to pull it off as cheaply as possible. We sanded the shop floors, my dad helped us paint the shop out, and random family members would swing by and help out with odd jobs that needed attention.

We couldn't decide on a colour, so we went with white everywhere.

We started to hit eBay, the *Trading Post* and auctions to pick up tables, chairs and kitchen equipment. (Our oven was a Blodgett that blew an element every time something big was on.) Gradually we inched closer to opening. We got the tick from the council, the shelves chopped and shunted from the vegie shop were now sitting in the kitchen, and the ingredients were gleaming, ready to go.

We opened not because we were ready, but because the money had run out. Teena was nailing the cakes, but I struggled. The problem was, finally *this* was to be our shop, and at last we were free to do our own thing — but what was that to be?

The social media critics pounced on our initially dismal and insipid selection and drove the knives deep. We stopped, had a few hissy moments with each other, and then just started cooking stuff that made us laugh, the customers cry, or that we were passionate about.

We were on the way.

THIS BEAUTIFUL BOOK

This book is an anarchic adventure into our minds and our shop. It is a bunch of things we are passionate about and love. That doesn't mean we will always make the same dishes: at some point they will change. It's a slice in time of our shop, as if the shop stood still for a summer and was bottled.

Have fun, cook with passion and because you love it, turn the music up loud and move to the beat. If you think it, try it. Just because you smile and have fun doesn't mean you are not a serious cook.

Lighten up, make a plan and get organised: pastry is about organisation, and that's about it. Chop and change recipes, and hopefully get inspired.

BUTTER MAKES IT BETTER

Since the shop opened, we have always made croissanty bits. The unmistakeable aroma of buttery oven-baked dough wafts along the street as Hobart begins to wake…

We are super lucky in Tasmania, as we have access to an amazing dairy company that churns butter and sells tasty milk and cream. Before we end up in an endless debate about why butter is better than margarine and have bloggers and large conglomerates sue us, our opinion is simply that butter tastes better.

Since the shop opened, we have always made croissanty bits. Every morning it reminds me a little of London, walking into the Connaught hotel to see Arlet, our baker, bobbing along with his fine backside, teasing strips of dough into their requisite shapes.

The unmistakeable aroma of buttery oven-baked dough wafts along the street as Hobart begins to wake. Often we get caught up in the rush of preparing the shop, but a short stroll to the fridge and soon enough the nostrils remember and the tastebuds begin to dance salaciously upon the tongue in anticipation.

There's an abundance of fresh fruit to slam on some rum babas (page 33), and fabulous local nuts to coax our daughter into eating something resembling healthy... although we're often left arguing on the stairs about the nutritional value of doughnuts.

If you are in search of a good croissant, look for the crumbs: the best croissants in Paris are the ones with the pigeons flocking around, ready to swoop on those flaky good bits.

Baking is all about organisation, so here is the big tip: once shaped, your hand-crafted croissants can be frozen until needed; our muffin batters can be made the day before; doughnuts can be kept in the fridge overnight, ready for frying at daybreak (just remember, if guests are staying with you overnight, to splash plenty of flour around in the morning so they appreciate all your apparent hard work, baking throughout the night).

Finally, we all know that some ingredients must come from overseas or the 'big island', but supporting a local farmer where you have the chance to walk amongst the beasts before they are milked is pretty special. It gives you a connection to your baked goods that makes them taste even better.

My favourite way to have croissants? Milk crate, astro turf, and bad pastry-chef-made coffee in the early morning light.

Croissants are the ultimate breakfast pastry — stuffed with chocolate, almonds, raisins or jam, dipped in coffee and sucked within an inch of their life before being gulped down. We never get sick of watching the croissants rise in the oven, as micro-thin layers of dough gently puff and turn golden. The best way to tell if you have made a good croissant is if you end up with all the flaky bits of pastry on the floor when you're eating it!

MAKES ABOUT 12

CROISSANTS

100 g (3½ oz) softened butter, plus 450 g (1 lb) cold butter
1 kg (2 lb 4 oz) strong flour
20 g (¾ oz) sea salt
100 g (3½ oz) sugar
80 g (2¾ oz) fresh yeast, or 40 g (1½ oz) active dried yeast (see tip)
1 egg, lightly beaten

It is preferable to start the dough the day before, as it will be easier to roll and turn; the dough also needs to be cold to take the butter.

In the bowl of a stand mixer fitted with a dough hook, combine the 100 g (3½ oz) of softened butter with the flour, salt, sugar, yeast and 550 ml (19 fl oz) of water. Mix to a firm dough, then wrap in plastic wrap and chill in the fridge overnight.

Pull out the dough and roll it out, on a lightly floured bench, into a large square about 2–3 cm (¾–1¼ inches) thick.

Place the 450 g (1 lb) of cold butter between two sheets of baking paper. Using a rolling pin, roll out the butter, to soften it to the same consistency as the dough. Then roll the butter into an even 1 cm (½ inch) sheet.

Incorporate the butter into the dough by placing the sheet of butter on top of the dough, in the centre. Now fold the corners of the dough in, as if making an envelope.

Turn the dough by rolling it out into a long strip about 2–3 cm (¾–1¼ inches) thick, then folding each end into the centre, then folding over again. Turn the dough 90 degrees between each turn, so the dough resembles a book, and the opening is to the right. The end result is a square of dough four layers thick.

You will need to repeat this rolling and turning process three times in total, resting the dough in the fridge for at least 1 hour between each go. Do not attempt to speed up the process by shortening the chilling times, or you'll end up with an inferior pastry.

Once all the turns are complete, roll the dough to 2.5 mm (1⁄16 inch) thick. Now cut the dough into 12 isosceles triangles, 8 cm (3¼ inches) across the base and 20 cm (8 inches) long.

Roll the dough into croissants, working from the base of each triangle, up to the pointy end.

Brush with the beaten egg, then cover and leave to prove in a warm place until slightly risen. This will take as long as it wants, as it will depend on the weather. Don't get too keen and bake your croissants too soon, or they'll split in all the wrong places.

Preheat the oven to 170°C (325°F/Gas 3). Spread the croissants on two baking trays and bake for 15 minutes, or until they are dark golden and nice and crispy.

CHILLED-OUT TIP

Once rolled and shaped, your unbaked croissants can be frozen until needed. Pull them from the freezer the night before and bake them just before you want to eat them. If you're planning on freezing the raw croissants, fresh yeast seems to work better than dried yeast as it is less temperamental.

Alrighty then, if you don't just want plain croissants, try these variations...

ALMOND CROISSANTS

Make a frangipane by melting 80 g (2¾ oz) of butter in a saucepan. Add 80 g (2¾ oz) of almond meal, 80 g (2¾ oz) of icing (confectioners') sugar, 2 eggs and 40 g (1½ oz) of plain (all-purpose) flour. Give a quick mix until smooth.

Smear the frangipane over the dough triangles, before rolling up and scattering with slivered almonds. Then smear a little more frangipane on top and dip in slivered almonds before proving and baking as before.

CHOCOLATE CROISSANTS

Cut a sheet of croissant dough into rectangles measuring about 10 x 13 cm (4 x 5 inches). Scatter with plenty of your favourite chocolate – such as chocolate melts (buttons) – before rolling the croissants up.

Classically in the industry we use specially made little chocolate sticks for these, but if you have a favourite chocolate or chocolate confectionery, use that instead and it will be the best chocolate croissant you've ever had. Prove and bake as before.

PAIN AUX RAISINS

Smear a sheet of croissant dough with frangipane (see the recipe for almond croissants, left) and scatter with slivered almonds, and raisins that have been soaked until plump in water, rum, orange juice or a liquid of your choice.

Roll up the dough like you're making chelsea buns or pinwheels. Slice into rings about 4 cm (1½ inches) thick. Prove and bake as before.

You can batch these into a cake tin and bake them together, but we find that they are best baked in individual pie moulds.

This recipe was Angela Hartnett's (Big Ange's) when we used to make these for the breakfast basket at the Connaught in London. By far and away, these are the best muffins I have ever made or eaten. The muffin batter gets better with age, so let it sit overnight at least. It lasts three days in the fridge, so you can bake the muffins as you need them. Be careful though — they are slightly addictive, so the batter does not normally make it past a second day.

MAKES 12

CARROT & ZUCCHINI MUFFINS

120 g (4¼ oz) caster (superfine) sugar
125 ml (4 fl oz/½ cup) vegetable oil
2 eggs
130 g (4½ oz) plain (all-purpose) flour
1 teaspoon baking powder
1 teaspoon bicarbonate of soda (baking soda)
1 teaspoon mixed (pumpkin pie) spice
a pinch of sea salt
100 g (3½ oz) grated carrot
100 g (3½ oz) grated zucchini (courgette)
50 g (1¾ oz) sultanas (golden raisins)
rolled (porridge) oats, for sprinkling

In a large bowl, mix the sugar, oil and eggs together until the sugar dissolves. Add the flour, baking powder, bicarbonate of soda, mixed spice and sea salt. Mix in the carrot, zucchini and sultanas. Cover and leave the mixture in the fridge for a while; overnight is best.

When you're ready to bake, preheat the oven to 200°C (400°F/Gas 6). Grease a 12-hole 125 ml (4 fl oz/½ cup) muffin tin.

Spoon the batter into the muffin holes, filling them about three-quarters full. Sprinkle with oats, then bake for 12–14 minutes, or until the muffins are a dark golden brown.

Leave to cool in the tin for a few minutes before turning out.

These muffins are best enjoyed while still warm, but will keep in an airtight container at room temperature for up to 3 days.

Every Sunday in New York we would walk up to the Bouchon Bakery and get one of these muffins and a sticky bun. We'd then head to Central Park to watch people being healthy and jogging. I felt pity for them: their Sunday was committed to making themselves better, and ours was about breakfast indulgence. Ironically, we never felt bad!

MAKES 12

BANANA WALNUT MUFFINS

3 bananas, roughly chopped
180 g (6 oz) caster (superfine) sugar
150 g (5½ oz) dark brown sugar
2 eggs
45 ml (1½ fl oz) vegetable oil
1 teaspoon sea salt
300 g (10½ oz) plain (all-purpose) flour, sifted
3 teaspoons baking powder
100 g (3½ oz) walnuts

CRUMBLE TOPPING

80 g (2¾ oz) butter
80 g (2¾ oz) caster (superfine) sugar
80 g (2¾ oz) plain (all-purpose) flour
1 teaspoon ground cinnamon

Preheat the oven to 180°C (350°F/Gas 4). Grease a 12-hole 125 ml (4 fl oz/½ cup) muffin tin, or line with paper cases.

Use an electric mixer to beat the banana, caster sugar and brown sugar to a smooth paste. Add the eggs, oil and salt and mix until combined.

Using a wooden spoon, fold in the flour, baking powder and walnuts, then dollop the batter into the muffin tins.

Combine the crumble topping ingredients and scatter over the top of the muffins.

Bake for 12–15 minutes, or until the crumble is golden. Leave to cool in the tin for a few minutes before turning out.

These muffins are best enjoyed while still warm, but will keep in an airtight container at room temperature for up to 3 days.

We had these buns at New York's Bouchon Bakery, and really wanted to recreate something similar for our shop. We tested and retested recipes, but failed to capture the bun's essence, so on our shop's opening day, we simply slammed some caramel in the bottom of our pie pans, then dressed the hot buns with even more caramel when we pulled them out of the oven, and voilà! This is the greatest pastry in the shop. It has everything you could ever want: sticky, salty, crispy, chewy, nutty, caramel. This recipe really needs to be started the day before.

MAKES 12

PECAN STICKY BUNS

CARAMEL

300 g (10½ oz) caster (superfine) sugar
100 g (3½ oz) liquid glucose
100 g (3½ oz) butter
5 g (⅛ oz) sea salt
300 ml (10½ fl oz) thin (pouring) cream

Place the sugar and glucose in a large heavy-based frying pan over medium heat. Cook, stirring occasionally, until the sugar has dissolved.

Increase the heat and cook the caramel for a few more minutes, until it is a dark amber colour. Once you have your desired colour, deglaze the pan by carefully adding the butter and salt, which will slow down the colour progression.

Remove from the heat and add the cream in a few additions – beware, at this stage the caramel likes to spit molten blobs of lava at you, so make sure you use a long spoon; using a big pan is also better insurance against spitting.

The caramel will keep in an airtight container for up to 1 week in the fridge or at cool room temperature.

DOUGH

75 g (2½ oz) softened butter, plus 300 g (10½ oz) cold butter
700 g (1 lb 9 oz) strong flour
55 g (2 oz) fresh yeast, or 23 g (1 oz) active dried yeast
75 g (2½ oz) sugar
2 teaspoons sea salt
6 egg yolks

It is preferable to start the dough the day before, as it will be easier to roll and turn; it also needs to be cold to take the butter.

In the bowl of a stand mixer fitted with a dough hook, combine the 75 g (2½ oz) of softened butter with the flour, yeast, sugar, salt, egg yolks and 400 ml (14 fl oz) of water. Mix to a firm dough, then wrap in plastic wrap and chill in the fridge overnight.

Pull out the dough and roll it out into a large square about 2–3 cm (¾–1¼ inches) thick.

Place the 300 g (10½ oz) of cold butter between two sheets of baking paper. Using a rolling pin, roll out the butter, to soften it to the same consistency as the dough. Then roll the butter into an even 1 cm (½ inch) sheet.

Incorporate the butter into the dough by placing the butter on top of the dough, in the centre. Now fold the corners of the dough in, as if making an envelope.

Turn the dough by rolling it out into a long strip about 2–3 cm (¾–1¼ inches) thick, then folding each end into the centre, then folding

»

»

over again. Turn the dough 90 degrees between each turn, so the dough resembles a book, and the opening is to the right. The end result is a square of dough four layers thick.

You will need to repeat this rolling and turning process three times in total, resting the dough in the fridge for at least 1 hour between each go.

Do not attempt to speed up the process by shortening the chilling times, or you'll end up with an inferior pastry.

SCHMEAR

200 g (7 oz) dark brown sugar
200 g (7 oz) butter
200 g (7 oz) almond meal
grated zest of 1 orange

Combine all the ingredients in a large bowl and mix to a smooth paste.

TO ASSEMBLE

500 g (1 lb 2 oz) pecans

Roll the dough into a large rectangle about 6 mm (¼ inch) thick.

Rub the schmear all over the dough, leaving about 5 cm (2 inches) free at the top end.

Add most of the pecans, and start rolling up from the bottom end; just before you complete the roll, brush the top edge with a little water to secure it to the roll. Cut the dough into 12 buns, about 4 cm (1½ inches) wide.

Grease twelve 10 cm (4 inch) metal pie tins. Add lashings of the caramel (but not all of it) and the remaining pecans. Place the buns in the tins and leave to prove in a warm place for 40 minutes, or until lightly risen.

Preheat the oven to 180°C (350°F/Gas 4).

Bake the buns for about 20 minutes, until they are golden brown and any excess caramel has begun to burn on the tray. Using tongs, flip the buns from the pie tins as soon as they leave the oven.

While still hot, brush with more caramel.

These buns are amazing still warm from the oven, but will keep in an airtight container at room temperature for several days.

Our daughter Matilda is being brought up in a sweet shop: this has led to her thinking that a chocolate croissant for breakfast with a 'babycino' is normal. Matilda rocks up to the shop before school, and sometimes trying to get her to eat something moderately healthy can be a challenge. We came up with this bar to trick her into believing it's a special treat. It works a charm and is great for grabbing on the go.

MAKES ABOUT 12 BARS

TILDA BARS

100 g (3½ oz) butter
220 g (7¾ oz) raw (demerara) sugar
120 g (4¼ oz) honey
2 Weet-Bix or other wheat cereal biscuits, crushed
100 g (3½ oz) dessicated (shredded) coconut
50 g (1¾ oz) pecans
100 g (3½ oz) dried apricots
180 g (6 oz) sultanas (golden raisins)
50 g (1¾ oz) raisins
100 g (3½ oz) rolled (porridge) oats
200 g (7 oz) Rice Bubbles or other puffed rice cereal
50 g (1¾ oz) sunflower seeds
50 g (1¾ oz) hazelnuts
50 g (1¾ oz) pumpkin seeds (pepitas)
50 g (1¾ oz) dried cranberries
75 g (2½ oz) plain (all-purpose) flour
½ teaspoon baking powder

Preheat the oven to 170°C (325°F/Gas 3). Line a 30 x 20 cm (12 x 8 inch) baking tray with baking paper.

Put the butter, sugar and honey in a saucepan and heat gently until warm.

Mix the remaining ingredients together in a large bowl and add the honey mixture.

At this stage, squeeze a little of the mixture in your hand to check it will hold together. You can add a little warm water to bind the mixture a bit more, if needed. It should hold together, but not be sticky.

Squash the mixture firmly into the baking tray.

Bake for 25 minutes, or until nice and golden. Remove from the oven and leave to cool for 5 minutes.

While still warm, cut into 12 bars, or any shape you like.

The bars will keep in an airtight container for up to 2 weeks.

We have started up our own little vigilante group, determined not to surrender to the world-wide 'cronut' craze. We've been making doughnuts from day one, but struggled to sell them with the usual jam filling. We tried a good many flavours, scouring the internet and discovering amazing doughnut houses, such as Voodoo Doughnut in Portland, Oregon. Finally we came up with a lemon meringue doughnut, filled with lemon curd and paying homage to those American cream-filled cakes, Twinkies.

MAKES 8–10

DOUGHNUTS

60 g (2¼ oz) fresh yeast, or 30 g (1 oz) active dried yeast
2 eggs
200 ml (7 fl oz) milk
65 g (2¼ oz) butter
65 g (2¼ oz) caster (superfine) sugar, plus extra for rolling
15 g (½ oz) sea salt
520 g (1 lb 2½ oz) plain (all-purpose) flour
vegetable oil, for deep-frying
your choice of filling, such as lemon curd (page 221), or a berry jam

Place the yeast, eggs, milk, butter, sugar, salt and flour in the bowl of a stand mixer with a dough hook attached. Mix at medium speed for about 5 minutes, or until you have a smooth silky dough.

Cover and set aside to prove in a warm place for about 45 minutes, or until doubled in size.

Divide the dough into portions of about 100 g (3½ oz) each. Mould into bun shapes and set aside on a greased baking tray. Leave to prove for another 20 minutes, or until doubled in size.

Fill a deep-fryer or large heavy-based saucepan half full with vegetable oil. Heat the oil to 165°C (330°F).

Add the doughnuts in two batches and cook for about 5 minutes on each side, or until dark golden.

Once cool, roll the doughnuts in extra sugar and fill with your choice of filling. Do this by making a small hole in the side of each one with the handle of a wooden spoon, then squeezing in some filling using a piping (icing) bag.

The doughnuts are best enjoyed same day.

These amazing little numbers arose after the second wave of 'cronut' disciples began begging us for a remake. We refused and instead baked some humble doughnuts, clad them in a thin veil of caramel, then dredged them in nuts or coated them in crispy, smoked animal flesh, before filling them with a flavoured cream. The idea was inspired by Spanish super-chef Ferran Adrià (of elBulli fame) and his 'golden egg': ours is a clumsy breakfasty knock-off, but the intriguing contrast of crunchy exterior and creamy centre has a certain romance.

MAKES 8–10

AMAZEBALLS

1 quantity of dough from the doughnuts recipe (page 29)
200 g (7 oz) caster (superfine) sugar
20 g (3/4 oz) butter
1 egg, lightly beaten
1 handful of roasted almonds or crisp-fried bacon
never-fail pastry cream (page 225), for filling
maple syrup or honey, for drizzling

Prepare and prove the doughnuts as directed on page 29, but do not deep-fry them.

Preheat the oven to 180°C (350°F/Gas 4). Place the sugar in a heavy-based frying pan over medium heat. Cook, stirring occasionally, until the sugar has dissolved.

Increase the heat to high and cook for a few more minutes, until the caramel is a dark amber colour. Once you have your desired colour, deglaze the pan by carefully stirring in the butter.

Pour the caramel onto a chopping board lined with baking paper, then smooth out with a palette knife until thin. Using a greased knife, quickly cut into 7 cm (2 3/4 inch) squares. (If it becomes too brittle, you can always warm the caramel in the oven to make it pliable again.)

Brush the buns lightly with the beaten egg. Bake for 12 minutes, or until they turn a lovely dark golden colour.

Place a square of caramel on top of each bun. Flash in the oven until the caramel has melted over the buns. Now sprinkle with almonds or bacon or any other goodies you feel worthy.

Leave to cool, before stuffing with pastry cream, and drizzling with honey for the almonds, or maple syrup for the bacon.

The amazeballs are best enjoyed same day.

I obtained this recipe from one of the most talented pastry chefs that I ever worked with — pastry phenomenon, Michael Rispe. It happens to be the easiest baba to make, and while most would say, 'Not for breakfast!', we find that a little baba with rum, torn peaches and fresh cream in summer really hits the spot.

MAKES 12

RUM BABAS

BABAS

125 ml (4 fl oz/½ cup) milk
30 g (1 oz) fresh yeast, or 15 g (½ oz) active dried yeast
4 eggs
75 g (2½ oz) melted butter
250 g (9 oz) plain (all-purpose) flour
1 teaspoon sea salt
20 g (¾ oz) currants
cream and fresh fruit, to serve

Warm the milk and add the yeast. Set aside for about 5 minutes to allow the mixture to get all foamy. Mix the eggs and melted butter into the yeasty milk.

Combine the flour, salt and currants in a separate large bowl, then add the milk mixture. Now with your hand – yes, your hand! – mix lightly to just bring the mixture together. Cover and set aside in a warm place for about 45 minutes, or until doubled in size.

Fill a piping (icing) bag with the mixture, then half-fill twelve 100 ml (3½ fl oz) greased dariole moulds. Set aside again in a warm place for another 20 minutes, or until the dough has risen to the top of the mould.

Preheat the oven to 180°C (350°F/Gas 4). Bake the babas for 15 minutes, then unmould. While the babas are cooling, prepare the soak.

SOAK

200 ml (7 fl oz) orange juice
grated zest of 1 orange
½ vanilla bean, cut in half lengthways, seeds scraped
100 g (3½ oz) panela or raw (demerara) sugar
100 ml (3½ fl oz) decent rum

Put all the ingredients in a saucepan with 500 ml (17 fl oz/2 cups) of water and heat until just warm. Please do not boil off the alcohol – that would be a waste!

Soak the cooled babas in the mixture for 2–3 minutes, or until doubled in size.

Once soaked, the babas can be kept in the fridge overnight, drizzled with the remaining soak so they don't dry out.

Just before serving, add an extra splash of rum to each baba to help them on their way.

Serve with cream and fresh fruit.

BABAS TO GO

The babas can be baked ahead and frozen for up to 2 weeks. Bake them as directed, but don't soak them. Pull them out of the freezer as needed, let them thaw, then soak them in the rummy orange juice mixture before serving.

ALBERT
PRODUCTIONS
IT'S A LONG

ELEVENSIES

We can't compete with the big bakers and their thousands of pie pallets — nor do we want to. All our pies are hand formed, and the filling doted upon like the youngest sibling in a large family.

A British institution, the partaking of 'elevensies' is a way of punctuating the morning with a fortifying little treat, to break the monotony of the long hours spent at work... or a quaint Hobbity ritual that adds refreshment to the morning. While our spelling is non-conformist, let it free you to partake of these morsels at any time of day.

We have always made a few pies and sausage rolls to try to soothe the customers who complain about the over-abundance of sweeties, and also to pick up a few punters who want the whole experience of being at Sweet Envy to be clad in butter, savoury or sweet.

At football and other sporting matches, one cannot barrack effectively without lubricating one's gullet with a bag of pastry-encrusted flesh and a warm flat beer. But the days of the pie are changing, and slowly the mega-factories are opening up a market for better-cooked bespoke pie and sausage roll concoctions.

Pies define the Australian bakery mindset: on our overseas adventures we even remember pining for a traditional bag of 'ears and lips' (those bad cuts of meat that large manufacturers normally use in pies). Nowadays we read up on all the mega-trendy bakeries, find out what they are doing and have a crack at the flavour combinations ourselves. This is a great way to get the creative juices flowing, put our own spin on new ideas and end up with some pretty delicious results.

It's important to make the pastry from scratch, where possible. Slow braising also invites the use of many interesting meats and cuts: tongues and cheeks, rabbits and wilder beasts, whatever we can find. We can't compete with the big bakeries and their thousands of pie pallets. All our pies are hand formed, and the filling doted upon like the youngest sibling in a large family... but delicious is defined by the time taken to prepare the fillings.

While most of our pies are consumed around lunchtime, we recommend you eat them when you feel like it, be it breakfast or dinner. Get out the good sauce and indulge.

Before we opened our shop, everyone was talking about the sausage rolls made by Sydney's Bourke Street Bakery, so we had to Google to find out the story. This is our take on their iconic classic. The spice combination is perfect with lamb, and in Tasmania we grow some mighty fine-tasting beasts, so this one seemed like a natural.

MAKES 8

LAMB & HARISSA SAUSAGE ROLLS

1 onion, diced
olive oil, for pan-frying
1 teaspoon cumin seeds
1 teaspoon ground coriander
1 teaspoon caraway seeds
500 g (1 lb 2 oz) coarsely minced (ground) lamb shoulder
1 quantity of requesón (page 195), or 400 g (14 oz) ricotta cheese
3 tablespoons harissa paste
1 handful of curly parsley, roughly chopped
10 mint leaves, roughly chopped
3 spring onions (scallions), roughly chopped
100 g (3½ oz) dried currants
2 teaspoons sea salt
½ quantity of puff pastry (page 227)
1 egg, lightly beaten
chilli flakes, for sprinkling

In a frying pan, sauté the onion in a little olive oil over medium heat for about 5 minutes, or until golden. Add the spices and toast along with the onion. Once the spices are fragrant and the onion has softened, place in a bowl. Add the lamb and requesón, harissa, parsley, mint, spring onions, currants and sea salt. Mix thoroughly.

To check the seasoning, sauté a little piece of the mixture and taste it. If you want some more salt or harissa, add it now. (The meat mixture can be made a day ahead and refrigerated until required.)

Preheat the oven to 180°C (350°C/Gas 4). Line a baking tray with baking paper.

Roll the puff pastry into a rectangle about 80 cm (31½ inches) long and 10 cm (4 inches) wide. Using a piping (icing) bag without a nozzle, pipe a tube of meat next to the longest edge.

Moisten the exposed pastry with a little water. Roll the pastry over the sausage meat to encase it, overlapping the edges slightly.

Cut the sausage roll into eight portions. Place on the baking tray, seam side down, and end to end. Brush with beaten egg and scatter with chilli flakes, then bake for 15–20 minutes, or until golden brown.

Serve hot, with your favourite tomato sauce or relish.

IT'S
A LONG
WAY
TO THE
TOP
IF YOU WANNA
WANNA
ROCK
N'
TOP
WANNA

The use of ricotta cheese in our sausage rolls was a happy accident. The truth is, we slipped home mid-shift in New York one day and watched Martha Stewart making spaghetti and meatballs on TV, and we stole the idea from there. Using ricotta is so much better than adding eggs and breadcrumbs, even if the breadcrumbs are soaked in milk, as the ricotta keeps the sausage roll moist and makes it taste better.

MAKES 8

PORK & FENNEL SAUSAGE ROLLS

1 onion, diced
2 teaspoons fennel seeds, plus extra for sprinkling
olive oil, for pan-frying
1 quantity of requesón (page 195), or 400 g (14 oz) ricotta cheese
100 g (3½ oz) slivered almonds
500 g (1 lb 2 oz) fatty, coarsely minced (ground) pork
3 spring onions (scallions), coarsely shredded
1 handful of curly parsley, coarsely shredded
5 sage leaves, coarsely shredded
2 teaspoons ground fennel
2 teaspoons sea salt
1 teaspoon freshly ground black pepper
½ quantity of puff pastry (page 227)
1 egg, lightly beaten

Preheat the oven 200°C (400°C/Gas 6). In a frying pan, sauté the onion and fennel seeds in a little olive oil over medium heat for about 5 minutes, or until the onion is golden. Transfer to a bowl and add the requesón.

Meanwhile, toast the almonds in the oven for 5 minutes, or until golden brown. Add the almonds to the onion mixture.

Turn the oven down to 180°C (350°C/Gas 4). Line a baking tray with baking paper.

Add the pork to the onion mixture, along with the spring onion, parsley, sage, ground fennel, sea salt and pepper. Mix thoroughly.

To check the seasoning, sauté a little piece of the mixture and taste it. If you want some more salt or pepper, add it now. (The meat mixture can be made a day ahead and refrigerated until required.)

Roll the puff pastry into a rectangle about 80 cm (31½ inches) long and 10 cm (4 inches) wide. Using a piping (icing) bag without a nozzle, pipe a tube of meat next to the longest edge.

Moisten the exposed pastry with a little water. Roll the pastry over the sausage meat to encase it, overlapping the edges slightly.

Cut the sausage roll into eight portions. Place on the baking tray, seam side down, and end to end. Brush with beaten egg and scatter with extra fennel seeds, then bake for 15–20 minutes, or until golden brown.

Serve hot, with your favourite sauce or relish.

I am not a vegetarian and am often left wondering why one would forgo delicious mouthfuls of succulent, moreish meat. As a carnivore, my standard has always been that if a meal must be vegetarian, its success will be determined by how much I pine for protein. Occasionally you get it right, and life does not get much better than this pastry-encrusted delight: portable cauliflower cheese.

MAKES ONE 22 CM (8½ INCH) PIE, OR SIX 10 CM (4 INCH) PIES

CAULIFLOWER CHEESE PIE

1 onion, diced
½ a leek, white part only, chopped
2 garlic cloves, crushed
olive oil, for pan-frying
½ a cauliflower, cut into florets
500 ml (17 fl oz/2 cups) milk
50 g (1¾ oz) butter
50 g (1¾ oz) plain (all-purpose) flour
50 g (1¾ oz) grated cheddar cheese, plus extra for scattering
50 g (1¾ oz) goat's cheese, crumbled
2 teaspoons sea salt
1 teaspoon freshly ground black pepper
½ quantity of savoury shortcrust pastry (page 227)

In a saucepan, sauté the onion, leek and garlic in a little olive oil over medium heat for about 5 minutes, or until the onion is golden.

Add the cauliflower, along with the milk. Bring to a simmer and cook, uncovered, for 10 minutes, or until the cauliflower is tender.

Strain the liquid through a colander, into a jug. Reserve the warm liquid, ready for the sauce. Reserve the cauliflower and leek mixture for the filling.

Melt the butter over medium heat, then add the flour and cook, stirring, for 1 minute. Add the warm liquid in a few additions, returning it to the boil each time. Remove from the heat and add the cheeses and reserved cauliflower mixture, along with the salt and pepper.

Pour into a bowl, cover the surface with plastic wrap to stop a skin forming, then cool in the fridge. (The sauce and cauliflower can be cooked a day ahead; the sauce is best used cold, as you don't want the cheese to boil in the oven.)

Preheat the oven to 180°C (350°C/Gas 4).

Roll out the pastry to about 3 mm (⅛ inch) thick and use it to line a 22 cm (8½ inch) flan (tart) tin, or six 10 cm (4 inch) pie tins. Line the pastry with baking paper and some baking beads or raw rice. Bake for 20 minutes, or until the pastry is golden brown.

Remove the baking paper and rice. Spoon in the cauliflower mixture, top with some more cheese and bake for 10 minutes, or until the cheese is golden brown. Serve hot.

ANCHOVY SAUCE
A Distinguished Recipe From
GEO WATKINS
PLAF!
OUF!
CHASSE GARDÉE DANGER!
PAN!...PAN!
HEIN?
ÇA S'ADRESSE AUX HOMMES, PAS À MOI!
ATTENTION! PIÈGES À LOUPS
CLAC
COIN!
PARIS

I have nightmares about fish pie from the days when the staff-meal chefs cleaned all sorts of C-grade, vile, stinking, slime-ridden, heathen, swamp-dwelling fish, and passed these off as sustenance to an overworked team of vitamin D-deficient fluorescent-tanned chefs. So I had to make fish pie real again — and pork neck brings a little something special to the party.

SERVES 4–6; MAKES ONE 22 CM (8½ INCH) PIE

PIG FISH PIE

FILLING

500 g (1 lb 2 oz) firm white fish fillets, cut into 4 cm (1½ inch) cubes
60 g (2¼ oz) sea salt
olive oil, for pan-frying
1 onion, roughly chopped
1 celery stalk, roughly chopped
½ a leek, white part only, roughly chopped
500 g (1 lb 2 oz) pork neck
1 bay leaf
5 black peppercorns
1 litre (35 fl oz/4 cups) milk, approximately
60 g (2¼ oz) butter
60 g (2¼ oz) plain (all-purpose) flour

Toss the fish and salt in a glass bowl. Cover and place in the fridge while braising the pork.

Heat some olive oil in a large saucepan and lightly sauté the onion, celery and leek over medium heat for about 5 minutes. Transfer the vegies to a bowl.

Put the pork neck in the saucepan and brown it all over. Return the vegies to the pan, along with the bay leaf, peppercorns and sufficient milk to cover. Bring to a simmer, cover with a round of baking paper and cook until the pork is tender – normally around 3 hours. Remove the pork neck from the milk, reserving the milk in the pan, and roughly chop it.

Remove the fish from the fridge; rinse and pat dry. Add it to the pan of milk, along with the chopped pork. Combine the butter and flour to make a paste, then add to the pan.

Bring the pie mixture to the boil very briefly to cook the flour. Pour into a 22 cm (8½ inch) baking dish, then cover and allow to chill. (The mixture can be made up to a day ahead.)

POTATO MASH

1 kg (2 lb 4 oz) floury potatoes, such as kennebec, scrubbed but not peeled
250 ml (9 fl oz/1 cup) thin (pouring) cream
100 g (3½ oz) butter, plus a little extra melted butter, for brushing

Preheat the oven to 180°C (350°C/Gas 4).

Spread the potatoes on a baking tray and bake for about 1 hour, or until cooked through.

While the potatoes are still hot, remove the skins. Reserve two potatoes, then mash the rest with the cream and butter. Season to taste.

TO ASSEMBLE

Preheat the oven to 180°C (350°C/Gas 4). Spread the mash over the cold pie filling. Slice the two reserved potatoes as thinly as possible and arrange on top of the mash, in overlapping concentric circles. Brush with melted butter.

Bake for 25–30 minutes, or until the potatoes are brown and the pie filling begins to bubble around the edges.

Ah pasties, the back-up snack at London's Victoria Station whenever the queue was too long at the souvlaki stand. We ate so many pasties we really missed them when we got home. Now, when we get the urge, we make them and have a quiet moment of reflection on times past. We keep this version simple, in the tradition of good pasties: plenty of potato and swede, and minimal spicing.

MAKES 8

TIDDLY OGGY

olive oil, for pan-frying
500 g (1 lb 2 oz) hogget, mutton or lamb, diced
1 onion, sliced
500 ml (17 fl oz/2 cups) chicken stock
1 swede (rutabaga), roughly chopped
a pinch of ground mace
8 waxy potatoes, peeled and roughly chopped (we use Tasmanian 'pink eye' potatoes)
60 g (2¼ oz) plain (all-purpose) flour
60 g (2¼ oz) butter
1 quantity of savoury shortcrust pastry (page 227)

Heat a splash of olive oil in a heavy-based saucepan. Sauté the meat over medium-high heat until browned all over.

Stir in the onion, stock, swede and mace and season with sea salt and freshly ground black pepper. Cover with a round of baking paper and simmer over low heat for about 2 hours, until the meat is tender.

Add the potato and cook for another 15 minutes, or until the potato is soft.

Combine the flour and butter to form a paste. Add to the saucepan and cook for 5 minutes, or until thickened. Pour the mixture into a heatproof dish, then cover and chill in the fridge for a good hour or so. (The mixture can be made a day or so ahead.)

Preheat the oven to 180°C (350°C/Gas 4). Line a baking tray with baking paper.

Roll out the pastry to about 3 mm (⅛ inch) thick. Use a side plate to cut out eight circles. Spread the filling over one half of the pastry, leaving a border. Fold the other pastry half over the filling and crimp the edges together.

Place the pasties on the baking tray and bake for 25–30 minutes, or until golden and delicious.

Well, well, Mrs Potter. This is our favourite pie to torment the punters at Easter, watching them squirm as they devour the Easter bunny. We add a layer of mushrooms sautéed with bacon, in homage to Beatrix and her mischievous friend.

SERVES 4–6; MAKES ONE 22 CM (8½ INCH) PIE

BEATRIX POTTER PIE

- 2 rabbits, legs and loins left whole, carcass chopped
- 2 bay leaves
- 3 parsley stalks
- 120 g (4¼ oz) butter
- olive oil, for pan-frying
- 1 carrot, diced
- 1 onion, diced
- 1 celery stalk, diced
- 2 garlic cloves, chopped
- 3 thyme sprigs
- 60 g (2¼ oz) plain (all-purpose) flour
- 100 g (3½ oz) bacon, roughly chopped
- 300 g (10½ oz) mushrooms, roughly chopped
- 1 quantity of savoury shortcrust pastry (page 227)
- 1 quantity of puff pastry (page 227)
- 1 egg, lightly beaten

Preheat the oven to 200°C (400°C/Gas 6). Spread the rabbit bones on a baking tray and roast for 10 minutes, or until dark. Turn the oven down to 100°C (200°C/Gas ½).

Drop the bones into a saucepan with the bay leaves, parsley stalks and 500 ml (17 fl oz/ 2 cups) of water. Cover with a round of baking paper and bring to a simmer. Bubble away for 1 hour to make a stock.

Meanwhile, place the rabbit loins in a small baking dish. Dot with 60 g (2¼ oz) of the butter, cover with a piece of baking paper and bake for 15 minutes, or until opaque.

Heat a splash of olive oil in a saucepan and brown the legs of the rabbit to seal them. Remove and set aside.

Now sauté the carrot, onion, celery and garlic for about 10 minutes, until light brown.

Strain the stock and add to the saucepan. Add the rabbit legs and thyme and season to taste with sea salt. Simmer for about 2½ hours, until the meat falls off the bone.

Strain the liquid through a colander, reserving the liquid. Pick the meat from the bones, then add it back to the saucepan, along with any salvageable vegetables and the liquid. Return to the heat.

Roughly chop the rabbit loins and add to the pan. Combine the remaining 60 g (2¼ oz) of butter and the flour. Add to the saucepan, mixing well, and cook for 5 minutes to thicken the sauce. Check the seasoning, then transfer to a bowl, cover and cool in the fridge for about 1 hour, or overnight if desired.

In a frying pan, sauté the bacon and mushrooms until the bacon is crispy. Reserve until ready to top the pie.

Line a 22 cm (8½ inch) pie tin with the shortcrust pastry, leaving some overhanging the edge. Add the filling and top with the sautéed mushrooms and bacon. Top with puff pastry, crimp the edges together and trim. Rest the pie for about an hour in the fridge.

Preheat the oven to 180°C (350°C/Gas 4).

Brush the pie with the beaten egg, then bake for 25–30 minutes, or until golden and delicious.

My favourite pie! I love the name, and the looks of horror as new customers squeal with disbelief when we confirm that yes, it really is 'tongue and cheek'. I like to think of this pie as a beggar's version of beef bourguignon — the only problem is, it's even better! It's best to start this pie the day before, marinating the beef cheeks in the red wine overnight.

MAKES ONE 22 CM (8½ INCH) PIE, OR SIX 10 CM (4 INCH) PIES

TONGUE & CHEEK

4 beef cheeks
300 ml (10½ fl oz) red wine
olive oil, for pan-frying
1 onion, diced
1 garlic bulb, cloves diced
½ a carrot, diced
½ a celery stalk, diced
½ a smoked ox tongue (you may need to order this ahead from your favourite butcher)
1 litre (35 fl oz/4 cups) chicken stock
1 teaspoon anchovy sauce
2 thyme sprigs
2 rosemary sprigs
6 black peppercorns
45 g (1½ oz) plain (all-purpose) flour
45 g (1½ oz) butter
1 quantity of savoury shortcrust pastry (page 227)
1 quantity of puff pastry (page 227)
1 egg, lightly beaten

Remove any big, thick, silvery bits of sinew from the beef cheeks and feed them to the dog. Dice the beef cheeks into bite-sized chunks. Marinate in the red wine overnight in the fridge.

Drain the beef, reserving the wine. Heat a little olive oil in a frying pan and sauté the beef over medium-high heat until caramelised all over. Transfer to a saucepan.

Using the same frying pan, sauté the onion, garlic, carrot and celery for 10 minutes, or until tender. Transfer to the saucepan.

Pour the reserved wine into the frying pan and cook until reduced by two-thirds, skimming off the impurities with a strainer as you go.

Peel the leathery external skin off the tongue. Dice the meat and add to the saucepan, along with the reduced red wine, stock, anchovy sauce and aromatics. Cover with a round of baking paper and simmer over low heat for about 3 hours, or until the meat is tender.

Combine the flour and butter. Add to the saucepan and continue to cook for about 5 minutes, until you cannot taste the flour. Check the seasoning, as the mixture may need a little more salt. Transfer the filling to a tray, cover and chill in the fridge for about 1 hour, until cold.

Go for the classic feel: line a 22 cm (8½ inch) flan (tart) tin, or six 10 cm (4 inch) pie tins, with the shortcrust pastry, leaving some to overhang the edge. Add the filling and top with puff pastry. Crimp the edges together and trim. Now rest the pie or pies for about an hour in the fridge.

Preheat the oven to 180°C (350°C/Gas 4).

Brush the pastry with beaten egg, then bake the pie or pies for 25–30 minutes, or until golden and delicious.

At home, this dish is a staple for Easter, and any other occasion we get to pull it together. As with beef wellington, the hardest part is cooking the protein correctly. Back in London, at the Connaught, pastry chef Freddy had an awful day in which it seemed logical to bake this dish for 2 hours, in the hope of baking the pastry nicely all the way through. Forget the pastry, look after the fish — it costs more!

SERVES 8–10

TROUT EN CROUTE

CREPES

300 ml (10½ fl oz) milk
60 g (2¼ oz) plain (all-purpose) flour
1 egg
a pinch of sea salt

In a bowl, whisk together all the ingredients. Cover the batter and rest in the fridge for at least 1 hour.

Heat a 22 cm (8½ inch) non-stick frying pan over medium–low heat. Pour about 60 ml (2 fl oz/¼ cup) batter into the pan and swirl to coat the pan in a thin, even layer (you want the crepes to be as thin as possible). When browned underneath, flip the crepe and briefly cook the other side, just to set the batter. Place on a sheet of baking paper.

Cook the remaining batter in the same way, stacking the crepes between layers of baking paper. You'll need five crepes all up. (The crepes can be made a day ahead and refrigerated until required.)

FILLING

12 baby leeks, trimmed
40 g (1½ oz) butter
4 silverbeet (Swiss chard) leaves, including the white stems, shredded
olive oil, for pan-frying
zest and juice of 1 lemon

Preheat the oven to 150°C (300°C/Gas 2). Wash the leeks thoroughly, then place on a non-stick baking tray. Dot with the butter and season with a little sea salt and freshly ground black pepper. Cover with foil and bake for 20 minutes, or until really tender. Cool and set aside.

Meanwhile, sauté the silverbeet in a frying pan in a splash of olive oil for about 2 minutes. Add the lemon zest and juice; this will help wilt the leaves. Cool and set aside.

TO ASSEMBLE

2 skinless ocean trout fillets, each about 30 cm (12 inches) long, pin-boned
1 quantity of puff pastry (page 227)
1 egg, lightly beaten

Place a large sheet of baking paper on the bench. Overlap the crepes on the paper, side by side, in one long line. Try to aim for your row of crepes to be about 40 cm (16 inches) long – the same length as the pastry you are going to roll out.

Place a layer of leeks along the centre of the crepes. Place the trout fillets on top, and season head to tail. Top with the cooled silverbeet. Now use the baking paper to help roll the fish up in the crepes.

Roll out the pastry into a rectangle about 40 cm (16 inches) long, 30 cm (12 inches) wide, and about 3 mm (⅛ inch) thick. Now cut the pastry in half lengthways, so you end up with two pieces 15 cm (6 inches) wide and 40 cm (16 inches) long.

Place the crepe-wrapped fish on top of one of the pieces of pastry. Brush the edge of the pastry with beaten egg, then top with the second piece of pastry. Crimp the edges together and rest in the fridge for at least 1 hour. (The dish can be assembled a day ahead and refrigerated until ready to cook.)

Preheat the oven to 200°C (400°C/Gas 6). Put the whole ensemble on a large baking tray. Brush the pastry all over with more beaten egg and score with a sharp knife. Slip the beauty into the oven and bake for 20 minutes.

To check if the fish is cooked, insert a small knife into the centre and then carefully hold it against your lip – if the knife feels warm, it's done.

CANDY BAR

Here are some of our bon bon trolley favourites from our days in New York. These are the candy bar treats that we still love, and that have made it into our shop.

At Gordon Ramsay's restaurants in New York, the crowning glory of the pastry kitchen was the bon bon trolley.

A thing of beauty, the bon bon trolley chinkled its way around the room, laced in gilt silver, holding seven Waterford crystal jars, tiers of delicate chocolates and hand-wrapped candies, whisked to each table for guests to devour as they sipped their after-dinner beverages.

We'd landed in New York two days before the soft opening of The London and Maze restaurants, where I was to be the executive pastry chef, and Teena sous chef. We were in a right tizz. My visa had been endlessly delayed, we had nowhere to live, and the pressure to perform was intense.

The opening of a restaurant involves months of planning, and we'd arrived to find everything in a clutter. We toured our yet-to-be-finished production kitchen to find stockpots boiling away and no air conditioning. Pastry-making was virtually impossible: the chocolate-tempering machine was tiny and more suited to the home cook than the demands of a large two-restaurant pastry kitchen.

Hastily we dug deep into our backlog of recipes and started churning out chocolates and confections as fast as we could to fill that magnificent bon bon trolley, even tempering chocolate in the champagne fridge to find a cool place to work, and storing our treasures in the vault-like wine store. Teena got a handle on the pastry-production kitchen, and fine-quality delights began to emerge.

For all the splendid beauties that bon bon trolley held, we went with the classics, trying to relive the childhood days of walking into the local candy bar to watch elderly ladies scoop delicious morsels from imposing jars.

A few months later, *The New Yorker* voted our bon bon trolley the best in New York! But we were not allowed to rejoice, not in public at least — pastry is the poor cousin to the chefs, so if they're getting slammed (and there was a bit of that), you do not celebrate.

But dance we did, in the kitchen's commercial walk-in fridge — our secret place to retreat and curse or celebrate without raising the ire of the crack squad.

Here are some of our bon bon trolley favourites from our days in New York... these are the candy bar treats that have made it into our shop. We love them for the fond memories they bring, of having made these in big cities, and of being a kid again.

These heavenly caramels adorned the very top of the bon bon trolley in New York City. There in a bowl of gilt silver they would totter, bouncing delicately from trolley top to guests' mouths. These are the real deal. If you have a salty caramel addiction and need to carry around a pocket of divine goodness, this recipe is for you.

MAKES ABOUT 30 PORTIONS

CHEWY SALTY CARAMELS

200 g (7 oz) caster (superfine) sugar
30 g (1 oz) liquid glucose
160 g (5½ oz) salted butter
100 ml (3½ fl oz) thin (pouring) cream
½ teaspoon sea salt

Line a 20 x 30 cm (8 x 12 inch) tray with baking paper and spray with cooking oil.

Place the sugar and glucose in a heavy-based saucepan and cook over medium heat for about 5 minutes, until you get a caramel that begins to foam up the side of the pan.

Add the butter and be careful as you stir, because the sugar has a tendency to spit molten lumps of caramel at you.

Add the cream and salt and return to the boil. Continue to cook until you reach 121°C (250°F) on a sugar thermometer.

Pour the caramel into the baking tray and leave to set overnight.

Turn out the caramel onto a chopping board and cut into 2 x 3 cm (¾ x 1¼ inch) pieces using a lightly greased knife.

Wrap individually in cellophane and twist the ends. (If you struggle to find cellophane, your local florist can normally supply some that is thin enough to twist.)

The caramels will keep in an airtight container for 2–3 weeks.

This is the first fruit jelly we ever made successfully. We used to roll the jelly delicately in acidic yoghurt powder for a truly weird flavour explosion. This recipe works equally well with other fruit purées, such as raspberry or blackcurrant. My absolute favourite is blackcurrant, as it reminds me of those blackcurrant jubes of my childhood — only these ones taste much better.

MAKES ABOUT 30 PORTIONS

APRICOT & LEMONGRASS PÂTE DE FRUITS

500 ml (17 fl oz/2 cups) apricot purée
1 lemongrass stem, bruised
550 g (1 lb 4 oz) caster (superfine) sugar, plus extra for coating
12 g (1⁄3 oz) pectin jaune
70 g (2½ oz) liquid glucose
1 teaspoon citric acid

Heat the apricot purée and lemongrass in a saucepan. Remove from the heat and leave to infuse in the pan for 10 minutes. Pass the mixture through a fine sieve, then return the purée to the pan.

Mix 50 g (1¾ oz) of the sugar with the pectin and add to the purée. Mix thoroughly and return to the boil. Add the remaining sugar and the glucose. Continue to cook to 170°C (338°F) on a sugar thermometer, then add the citric acid.

Pour the mixture into a greased 20 x 30 cm (8 x 12 inch) tray and allow to set overnight.

Portion into bite-sized pieces, then roll in extra sugar to coat.

The pâte de fruits will keep in an airtight container for 2–3 weeks.

Many Australians have fond memories of their dads dragging them into Darrell Lea confectionery shops to gather soft liquorice and peanut brittle. In the lead-up to our New York restaurant debut, we had the task of filling loads of Waterford crystal jars for the bon bon trolley, and this brittle fitted the bill perfectly — although I seem to remember our chef de cuisine losing a crown from his tooth whilst munching merrily. Eater, beware!

MAKES ABOUT 350 G (12 OZ)

PEANUT BRITTLE

120 g (4¼ oz) peanuts
200 g (7 oz) caster (superfine) sugar
25 g (1 oz) butter

Preheat the oven to 150°C (300°F/Gas 2). Spread the peanuts on a baking tray and roast for 5–10 minutes, or until golden.

Put the sugar and 100 ml (3½ fl oz) of water in a heavy-based saucepan. Slowly bring to the boil to dissolve the sugar.

Increase the heat and cook to a dark golden caramel colour – about 160°C (320°F) on a sugar thermometer; this will take about 10 minutes. Remove from the heat and add the butter.

Spread the roasted nuts over a silicon baking mat and pour the caramel over.

Place another silicon baking mat on top and use a rolling pin to make an even layer. Allow to cool.

Once set, break the peanut brittle into pieces. It will keep in an airtight container for up to 2 weeks.

SLINKY SILICON

If you don't have a silicon baking mat, you can use sheets of baking paper instead, but there are difficulties with using paper as the mixture sticks a bit. It's best to spend some money and get a silicon baking mat, as I'm sure making this recipe will not be a one-off!

When making honeycomb, there are two big tips. First, get that pan you were thinking of using, put it back in the cupboard and use the next size up — this is a frightfully hot mixture that will foam up the pan and burn you. Second, the bicarbonate of soda will continue to darken the caramel until it is cold, so don't be alarmed when this happens.

MAKES ABOUT 6–8 CUPS

HONEYCOMB

30 g (1 oz) honey
30 g (1 oz) golden syrup (or you can just use extra honey)
180 g (6 oz) caster (superfine) sugar
2 teaspoons bicarbonate of soda (baking soda), sifted

Place the honey, golden syrup, sugar and 30 ml (1 fl oz) of water in a large, deep saucepan. Bring to the boil and cook to a light caramel colour – about 155°C/310°F on a sugar thermometer; this will take about 10 minutes.

Add the sifted bicarbonate of soda and whisk lightly – the honeycomb will expand very quickly at this stage, so be careful.

Quickly, but gently, pour the mixture onto a silicon baking mat or greased tray, trying not to knock out the bubbles just created.

Once cool, bash apart into chunks.

The honeycomb will keep in an airtight container for up to 2 weeks.

DIP, SPRINKLE, CRUMBLE
The honeycomb is fabulous dipped in melted chocolate, sprinkled over rice pudding with fresh raspberries, or crumbled over ice cream and lashed with chocolate sauce.

Fudge: a noun, a verb, an interjection... and something delicious! Coated in chocolate, this creamy soft fudge is decadent and divine. You cannot stop at just one piece.

MAKES 12–15 PORTIONS

CHOCOLATE FUDGE

330 g (11½ oz) sugar
125 g (4½ oz) liquid glucose
50 ml (1½ fl oz) thin (pouring) cream
100 ml (3½ fl oz) milk
120 g (4¼ oz) soft fondant icing
225 g (8 oz) dark chocolate, chopped

Put the sugar, glucose, cream and milk in a large saucepan and bring to the boil. Cook, stirring occasionally, until it reaches 115°C (239°F) on a sugar thermometer.

Remove from the heat and leave to cool in the saucepan to 50°C (122°F).

Add the fondant and mix well before adding the chocolate, stirring vigorously to avoid lumps. There is no need to melt the chocolate, as the residual heat will do that for you.

Grease a 20 x 30 cm (8 x 12 inch) tray and line with baking paper. Pour in the fudge mixture. Allow to set overnight, then cut into portions.

The fudge will keep in an airtight container for up to 2 weeks.

WHITE CHOCOLATE FUDGE

Instead of the dark chocolate, use 275 g (9¾ oz) of white chocolate.

Marshmallow is a rite of passage, and once you make your own it becomes impossible to buy the pre-packaged, unloved stuff. So why not flavour-bend? Clad it with bacon and chocolate dip, and then the ultimate: place on a stick and toast over a fire.

MAKES 12–15 PORTIONS

MARSHMALLOW

270 g (9½ oz) caster (superfine) sugar
180 g (6 oz) liquid glucose
15 g (½ oz) powdered gelatine
cornflour (cornstarch), for dusting
icing (confectioners') sugar, for dusting

Put the sugar, glucose and 70 ml (2¼ fl oz) of water in a heavy-based saucepan. Bring to 122°C (251°F), using a sugar thermometer as a guide.

Remove from the heat and let the mixture cool in the pan to 100°C (212°F).

Put the gelatine in a heatproof bowl with 90 ml (3 fl oz) of cold water. Once the gelatine has soaked up all the water, place the bowl over a saucepan of hot water to melt the gelatine. Add the mixture to the hot syrup.

Transfer to the bowl of a stand mixer and whisk until light, fluffy and cool; this normally takes 6–7 minutes.

Grease a 20 x 30 cm (8 x 12 inch) tray and line with baking paper. Spread the marshmallow mixture over the tray.

Allow to set for several hours or overnight, before portioning and dusting with equal parts cornflour and icing sugar.

The marshmallows will keep in an airtight container for up to 3 days.

FLAVOUR BENDERS

Try adding these at the end, before spreading the marshmallow mixture on the tray.

BACON MAPLE SYRUP

100 g (3½ oz) crispy fried diced bacon pieces
50 ml (1¾ fl oz) maple syrup

FUZZY NAVEL

2 teaspoons orange blossom water
50 g (1¾ oz) toasted shredded coconut

LIME AND VANILLA

scraped seeds from 2 vanilla beans
zest of 1½ limes

Some have made soft nougat into an absolute art form. Personally, my biggest aversion to making nougat is the thought of getting everything ready, dirtying half the utensils in the kitchen, then having to clean them of their stickiness after making the intrepid beast. But it's worth it! My tip: make the mess and don't worry about the carnage, then throw everything in the laundry trough for a good, long soak before attempting the clean-up.

MAKES 12–15 PORTIONS

NOUGAT

200 g (7 oz) whole raw almonds
70 g (2½ oz) hazelnuts
100 g (3½ oz) pistachio nuts
230 g (8 oz) honey
380 g (13½ oz) caster (superfine) sugar
120 g (4¼ oz) liquid glucose
2 egg whites (50 g/1¾ oz)
150 g (5½ oz) white couverture chocolate
70 g (2½ oz) flaked almonds
75 g (2½ oz) dried apricots
75 g (2½ oz) dried cranberries
50 ml (1½ fl oz) vegetable oil

Preheat the oven to 170°C (325°F/Gas 3). Spread the almonds, hazelnuts and pistachios on a baking tray and roast for 10 minutes, or until lightly browned.

Turn off the oven and leave the nuts in the oven – they are easier to incorporate into the nougat mixture while they are warm.

In one saucepan, bring the honey to the boil and cook to 121°C (250°F) on a sugar thermometer.

In another saucepan, bring the sugar, glucose and 100 ml (3½ fl oz) water to 155°C (310°F).

Using electric beaters, whisk the egg whites to stiff peaks. Carefully add the honey, followed by the sugar syrup, pouring them down the side of the bowl to prevent the hot stuff flying out if it hits the whisk. Now whisk at high speed for about 6 minutes, to make a stiff meringue.

Melt 50 g (1¾ oz) of the chocolate, then add to the meringue and mix until emulsified. Sometimes the mixture looks like it has split; have faith and keep whisking, and the meringue will be transformed into a smooth, shiny mixture.

Add the toasted nuts, flaked almonds and dried fruit. Using the back of a spoon, quickly press into a greased 20 x 30 cm (8 x 12 inch) tray lined with baking paper. The mixture is usually quite hot at this point, so treat it like hot potatoes and move quickly! Allow to set for a few hours.

Roughly chop the remaining 100 g (3½ oz) of chocolate and melt in a heatproof bowl over a saucepan of simmering water. Add the oil and mix until fully combined.

Coat each side of the nougat with a thin layer of chocolate, before cutting into portions.

The nougat will keep in an airtight container for 2–3 weeks.

The first time we ever made caramelised popcorn was in London. Teena is the planner in our partnership, so this left me throwing popping corn into liquid caramel. Let's just say Teena was not too happy when corn and caramel splattered all over our studio apartment while we shielded ourselves behind the duvet. Luckily, by the time we took up our new jobs in New York, we'd had enough time to sleep on it and remedy our technical blunder.

MAKES ABOUT 8 CUPS

CARAMELISED POPCORN

400 g (14 oz) caster (superfine) sugar
8 cups freshly popped corn; you'll need about 250 g (9 oz) raw kernels
10 g (¼ oz) butter

Put the sugar and 100 ml (3½ fl oz) of water in a deep heavy-based saucepan – a low, wide saucepan is better than one that is narrow and high. Bring to the boil and cook to 121°C (250°F) on a sugar thermometer.

Using a 1 litre (35 fl oz/4 cup) jug, measure out exactly 8 cups of popcorn, adding it to the pan. Stir until the popcorn is coated and the sugar crystallises on the outside of the corn. Keep mixing it over the heat so the popcorn slowly begins to caramelise into an even golden colour; this will probably take about 10–15 minutes. You need to keep the popcorn moving at this stage as it can catch on the bottom of the pan and burn easily.

Remove from the heat and add the butter. Turn out onto greased trays and allow to cool.

The popcorn will keep in an airtight container for 2–3 weeks.

POPPING WITH FLAVOUR

We like to work in little flavour additions, normally after we've poured the popcorn onto the tray or bench to cool. (If you add the additions straight away, they will stick to the still-moist caramel.)

Try roasted nuts, peanut butter, chocolate chunks...

E 20

AFTERNOON DELIGHT

Nothing compares to taking a moment out with a cuppa. We try not to compete with the classics, but rather delve deep into their soul…

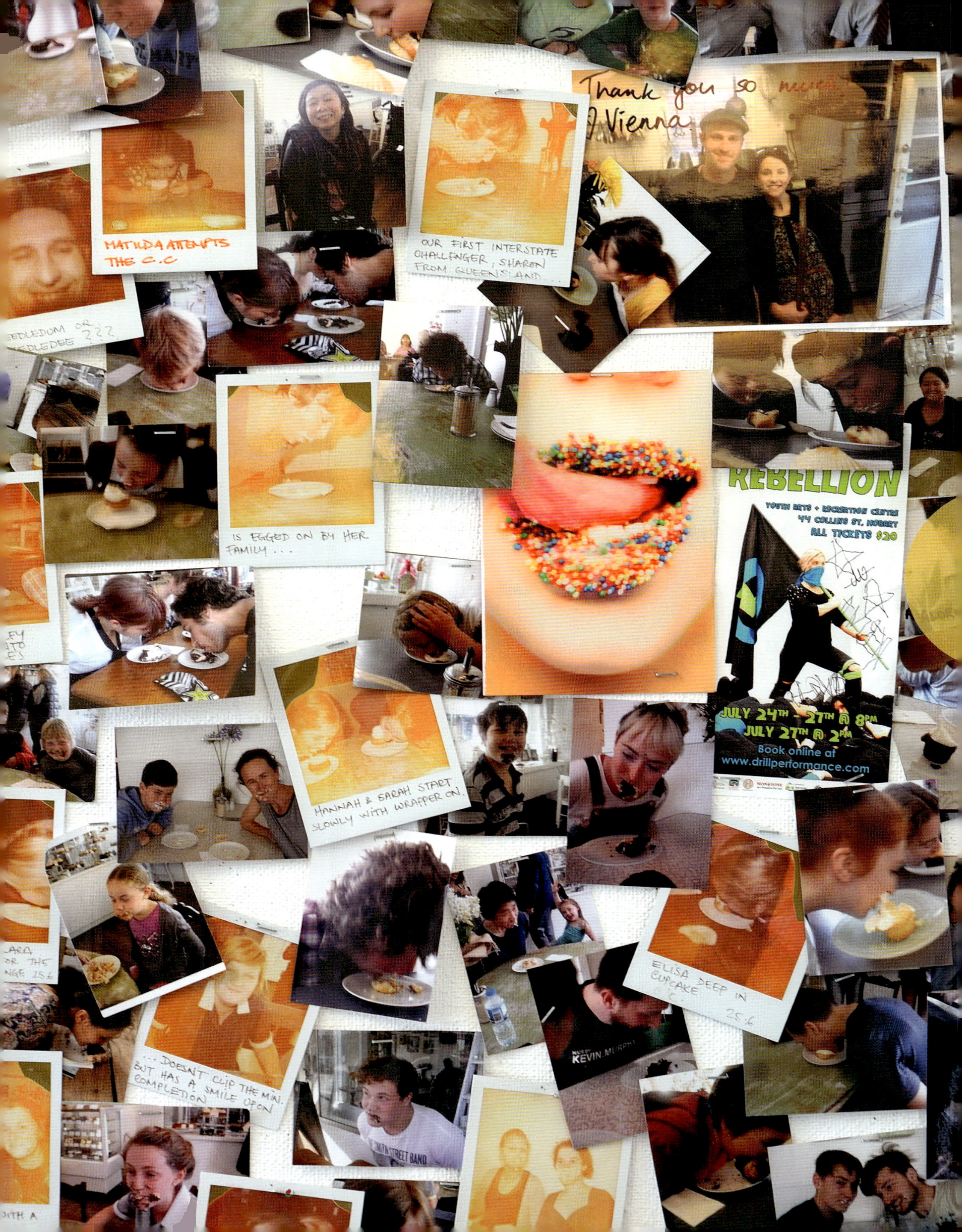
Thank you so
Vienna
MATILDA ATTEMPTS THE C.C
OUR FIRST INTERSTATE CHALLENGER, SHARON FROM QUEENSLAND
IS EGGED ON BY HER FAMILY...
REBELLION
YOUTH ARTS + RECREATION CENTRE
44 COLLINS ST, HOBART
ALL TICKETS $20
JULY 24TH - 27TH @ 8PM
JULY 27TH @ 2PM
Book online at
www.drillperformance.com
HANNAH & SARAH START SLOWLY WITH WRAPPER ON.
ELISA DEEP IN CUPCAKE
25:6
... DOESN'T CLIP THE MIN. BUT HAS A SMILE UPON COMPLETION
KEVIN.MURPHY

When we lived in London we found its legendary inclement weather quite acceptable. London is all about good tea and genteel rituals: a celebration of opaque skies and lazy afternoons snacking from stands laden with cakes and dainty biscuits.

There was a cracker of a 'greasy spoon' not far from where we lived in London. They had an amazing two-handled enamel teapot filled with tea that would gradually get more bitter and tannic as the day went on. Thank god for milk and sugar. Suck on a few dunked digestives, sink back into a well-worn chair and you have reached Elysium.

Real biscuits are evocative. There is something soothing about them, like being at your grandmother's house with the smell of roses wafting through the bedraggled screen door. The special teapot is drawn from brown-glass cabinets, and you are treated to tea and taught the proper way to drink, with the pinkie finger extended... The sheer simplicity of biscuits and their ability to morph with a little dunking into another texture and flavour makes them endlessly desirable.

Afternoon-tea stands are now laden with macarons and macaroons, tricky slices of layered French-style *entremets*, cupcakes with gravity-defying frosting, whoopie pies and ho-hos, ding dongs and ethereal tarts. I celebrate their place, but nothing compares to taking a moment out with a cuppa. We try not to compete with the classics, but rather delve deep into their soul to see if by chance we can find their true origins, before they became the mass-manufactured oddities sold in mega-marts.

Many über chefs have turned up their noses at the fact that we make cupcakes in our shop. The reality is that every day we are making butter cake for Teena to carve and coat in elaborate creations for special events, so to sling in a few cupcakes makes sense and adds to Teena's impressive cake cabinet, which fronts the shop.

Dave Osborne (Super Dave, friend and extreme barista) created our legendary 'cupcake challenge' and insanity was let loose upon the shop. Eat a cupcake in under a minute with no hands and it's yours! To date the fastest was 13 seconds, but we cannot comment as to whether that fine young lad ended up in intensive care with frosting on the brain.

These recipes are the ones that will send your sky rockets in flight and satisfy you for afternoon delight.

A caramel lover's delight — chocolate cookies with a runny caramel centre and creamy caramel frosting, dipped in milk chocolate. It took a while to find a name for this one, but while highway driving one day, we pulled up along a pimped prime mover that had the lady mud flaps that say, 'Bada bing!', so we stole it.

MAKES 12 BISCUITS

BADA BING!

CHOCOLATE COOKIES

160 g (5½ oz) pastry flour, sifted
40 g (1½ oz) Dutch-processed cocoa powder, sifted
60 g (2¼ oz) icing (confectioners') sugar, sifted
120 g (4¼ oz) butter
a pinch of sea salt
1 egg

Rub together the sifted flour, cocoa, icing sugar, butter and salt, to a fine crumb. Add the egg and mix as little as possible to bring the dough together. Wrap into 3–4 manageable portions and chill in the refrigerator for at least a couple of hours; the dough will easily keep for several days.

Preheat the oven to 180°C (350°C/Gas 4). Line two baking trays with baking paper.

Roll out the dough to about 3 mm (⅛ inch) thick and cut into 24 oblongs, about 3 x 10 cm (1¼ x 4 inches) in size.

Place on the baking trays and bake for about 10 minutes. It is difficult to tell if the dough is cooked, so gently try to move the biscuits on the tray; if they move easily, remove from the oven and cool on the tray.

TO ASSEMBLE

1 quantity of creamy vanilla frosting (page 231)
½ quantity of salty caramel (page 220)
450 g (1 lb) milk chocolate, chopped
50 ml (1½ fl oz) vegetable oil

Make the frosting and add 50 g (1¾ oz) of the salty caramel.

Pipe a ring of frosting around the edge of half the biscuits, then put a spoonful of the remaining salty caramel in the centre and pop a lid on top. Leave to firm for about 30 minutes.

Melt the chocolate in a heatproof bowl set over a saucepan of just simmering water, ensuring the base of the bowl doesn't touch the water. Add the oil and mix until fully emulsified.

Submerge the biscuits in the melted chocolate one at a time, draining off any excess, before placing them on a lined tray to set.

The biscuits will keep in an airtight container in a cool dark place for up to 1 week.

Take the good old Iced Vo-Vo, the iconic Australian biscuit of our grandparents' generation. Make it round instead of rectangular, pile on lots of fresh soft marshmallow, coconut and homemade raspberry jam, and I defy you to find a better biscuit for a cup of tea.

MAKES 12 BISCUITS

RO-VO

SUGAR COOKIE DOUGH

200 g (7 oz) pastry flour, sifted
60 g (2¼ oz) icing (confectioners') sugar, sifted
120 g (4¼ oz) butter
a pinch of sea salt
1 egg

Rub together the sifted flour, icing sugar, butter and salt, to a fine crumb. Add the egg and mix as little as possible to bring the pastry together. Wrap into 3–4 manageable portions and chill in the refrigerator for at least a couple of hours; the dough will keep for several days.

Preheat the oven to 180°C (350°C/Gas 4). Line a baking tray with baking paper.

Roll out the dough to about 3 mm (⅛ inch) thick, then cut into twelve 7 cm (2¾ inch) discs. Bake for 15 minutes, or until cooked through and golden brown. Remove from the oven and cool on the tray.

MARSHMALLOW

270 g (9½ oz) caster (superfine) sugar
180 g (6 oz) liquid glucose
15 g (½ oz) powdered gelatine

Put the sugar and glucose in a heavy-based saucepan with 70 ml (2¼ fl oz) of water. Bring to the boil and cook to the soft-ball stage (118°C/245°F on a sugar thermometer). Leave to cool to 100°C (212°F).

Put the gelatine in a heatproof bowl with 90 ml (3 fl oz) of cold water. After about 5 minutes, once the gelatine has soaked up all the water, place the bowl over a saucepan of hot water to melt the mixture briefly, then add it to the hot sugar syrup. Use hand-held electric beaters or an electric mixer with a whisk attachment to beat the marshmallow until light, fluffy and cool.

TO ASSEMBLE

100 g (3½ oz) desiccated (shredded) coconut
12 teaspoons raspberry jam

Pipe a ring of marshmallow around the edge of each biscuit. Dip each into the coconut and put a teaspoon of raspberry jam in the centre.

These biscuits are best eaten the next day, as the marshmallow gets a nice chewy stickiness to it.

MOON PIE MAGIC

To make moon pie biscuits, prepare as above, but pipe marshmallow around only six biscuits, then top each of these with a teaspoon of blackberry or boysenberry jam, instead of raspberry jam. Put the other biscuits on top and allow to firm for 30 minutes, then dip the biscuits in the melted chocolate mixture from the mit mats recipe on page 100.

The Carlton Club
KERSLAKE'S HOTEL

The Red Rose Cafe
LAUNCESTON
COLES
CAFE

We made these biscuits as part of the cookie plate at London's Connaught, and loved the almond and anise flavour combination. The best thing is to dunk them in some vin santo or other divine dessert wine, whilst sipping good espresso. Make sure you are sitting down, as this may very well change your life.

MAKES 30 BISCUITS

CANTUCCI

180 g (6 oz) butter
275 g (9¾ oz) caster (superfine) sugar
3 eggs, lightly beaten
2 teaspoons baking powder
1 teaspoon sea salt
500 g (1 lb 2 oz) pasta flour, sifted (see tip)
175 g (6 oz) whole almonds
1 teaspoon ground star anise

Preheat the oven to 200°C (400°C/Gas 6). Line a baking tray with baking paper.

Using electric beaters, cream the butter and sugar until pale and creamy. Add the eggs gradually. Add the baking powder, salt and sifted flour and mix until well combined, then fold in the almonds and star anise.

Put the mixture in a piping (icing) bag fitted with a large nozzle, or no nozzle. Pipe out into fingers, about 4–5 cm (1½–2 inches) wide and as long as your tray, straight onto the baking tray. Bake for 15 minutes, or until three-quarters baked.

Remove from the oven and cut the fingers on an angle into 1 cm (½ inch) slices. Place each slice back on the tray and bake for about 5 minutes more, or until golden brown all over. Remove from the oven and cool on the tray.

The biscuits will keep in an airtight container in a cool dark place for up to 2 weeks.

FLOUR POWER
You need to use pasta flour in these biscuits, rather than regular plain (all-purpose) flour, as it is higher in protein and gives a firmer texture. The flour is often labelled '00' on the packet.

Everyone has a cake that Mum or Gran made, which defines their childhood. Thanks to our daughter, the cake we make a lot is from the movie *Matilda*. (Old Trunchbull, what were you thinking? That cake you made Bruce eat looked so divine that the poor lad may have had a culinary gastronomic peak too soon, and lost his life to mediocre piffle for the rest of his days!) The buttermilk in this cake can be substituted with milk if you really want, BUT the flavour of the buttermilk really makes the cake go from good to divine.

MAKES ONE 20 CM (8 INCH) CAKE, OR 24 CUPCAKES

CLASSIC RICH BUTTERMILK CHOCOLATE CAKE

130 g (4½ oz) butter
225 g (8 oz) soft brown sugar
75 g (2½ oz) sugar
2 eggs
225 g (8 oz) plain (all-purpose) flour
75 g (2½ oz) Dutch-processed cocoa powder
2 teaspoons bicarbonate of soda (baking soda)
a pinch of sea salt
300 ml (10½ fl oz) buttermilk
3 teaspoons vanilla extract
2 quantities of chocolate frosting (page 231) or ganache (page 231)

Preheat the oven to 180°C (350°C/Gas 4). Line a 20 cm (8 inch) round cake tin with baking paper, or line two 12-hole 125 ml (4 fl oz/½ cup) muffin tins with paper cases.

Using electric beaters, cream the butter and sugars until pale and creamy. Slowly add the eggs one at a time, beating well each time.

Sift the flour, cocoa, bicarbonate of soda and sea salt together into a bowl. Add the mixture to the butter mixture in batches, alternating with the buttermilk and vanilla. With each addition, beat until the ingredients are incorporated, but do not overmix.

Pour the batter into the cake tin, or divide among the muffin holes. Bake the cupcakes for 20 minutes, and the cake for 30–35 minutes, or until a skewer inserted into the middle comes out clean.

Leave to cool in the tin or tins for 10 minutes, before turning out onto a wire rack to cool completely.

Once cooled, smother the top of the cake or cupcakes with the frosting or ganache.

The frosted cake or cupcakes will keep in an airtight container in a cool dark place for up to 2 days.

This is our version of the classic drizzle cake. Originally we made the recipe with oranges, but thanks to our good friend Laurrie we have a constant supply of beautiful lemons. We were going to make the traditional version, but in a moment of one-upmanship, wondered what would happen if we topped the beauty with caramel-crusted lemon slices and a thick drizzle of sticky, sharp and tangy lemon icing. Well, now we know.

MAKES ONE 22 CM (8½ INCH) CAKE

LEMON DRIZZLE

220 g (7¾ oz) caster (superfine) sugar
2 lemons, thinly sliced
375 g (13 oz) plain (all-purpose) flour
1 teaspoon baking powder
90 g (3¼ oz) polenta
3 eggs
125 g (4½ oz) crème fraîche or sour cream
250 g (9 oz) butter, melted
thick (double) cream, to serve

LEMON ICING

200 g (7 oz) icing (confectioners') sugar
grated zest and juice of 1 lemon

Preheat the oven to 180°C (350°C/Gas 4). Line a 22 cm (8½ inch) cake tin with baking paper.

Put the caster sugar in a heavy-based saucepan over medium heat and melt to make a caramel, tipping the pan from side to side occasionally. Pour the caramel into the cake tin to coat the bottom, then place the lemon slices around the base of the tin, in concentric circles.

Combine the flour, baking powder and polenta in a mixing bowl, making a well in the centre. Add the eggs and crème fraîche to the well, add the melted butter and stir until smooth and free of lumps.

Spoon the batter into the cake tin, onto the lemon slices. Bake for 50 minutes, or until a skewer inserted into the middle of the cake comes out clean.

Leave to cool in the tin for 10 minutes, before inverting onto a serving plate.

Once cooled, make the icing. Sift the icing sugar into a bowl, then mix in the lemon zest and juice to give a thickish icing. Spoon onto the top of the cake, make tea, find friends, and enjoy with dollops of thick cream.

The cake will keep in an airtight container in a cool dark place for 3–4 days; the un-iced cake can be frozen for up to 1 month.

Afternoon tea in London and New York was always a big hit: the highlight for us was having Ozzy Osbourne come into the kitchen and demand more of those 'Amazing scones, man!' So, we thought we should share these 'amazing scones' with everyone. Serve them while still hot, with loads of butter and homemade jam if you're a sinner — or for those who are proper and have the patience, wait until the scones are cold and serve them with clotted cream and berries. If you have a split personality and can't decide if you should be good or bad, toss a coin, as both are great.

MAKES 20 SCONES

SCONES

500 g (1 lb 2 oz) plain (all-purpose) flour
90 g (3¼ oz) caster (superfine) sugar
30 g (1 oz) baking powder
125 g (4½ oz) butter
1 egg
100 ml (3½ fl oz) cold milk, plus extra for brushing

In a bowl, using your fingertips, rub the flour, sugar, baking powder and butter to a fine crumble, but do not overmix at this stage. Add the egg and milk and mix to a smooth dough. Allow to rest for 10 minutes.

Meanwhile, preheat the oven to 200°C (400°F/Gas 6). Line two baking trays with baking paper.

Roll out the dough to about 4 cm (1½ inches) thick. Cut out discs using a 5 cm (2 inch) round cutter and place on the baking trays. Using a pastry brush, lightly brush with cold milk.

Bake for 10–15 minutes, or until the scones are golden and sound hollow when tapped.

The scones are best enjoyed the same day.

A salute to the great Kingston biscuit — another Australian favourite, consisting of two coconut biscuits sandwiched around a chocolate centre. Our version is slightly better: that's why it was given the name Margate. If you live in Tasmania, you will know why, but for the rest of you, it simply comes down to postcode: the little southern coastal town of Margate is just a few miles from the town of Kingston, but is considered way better.

MAKES 12 BISCUITS

MARGATES

130 g (4½ oz) butter
1 tablespoon golden syrup or honey
230 g (8 oz) sugar
120 g (4¼ oz) desiccated (shredded) coconut
120 g (4¼ oz) rolled (porridge) oats
2 teaspoons vanilla extract
2 teaspoons bicarbonate of soda (baking soda)
175 g (6 oz) pastry flour, sifted
a pinch of sea salt
½ quantity of creamy vanilla frosting (page 231)

GANACHE

150 g (5½ oz) dark chocolate, chopped
150 ml (5 fl oz) thin (pouring) cream

Preheat the oven to 180°C (350°C/Gas 4). Line two baking trays with baking paper.

In a large saucepan, gently melt the butter and golden syrup, then add the sugar, coconut, rolled oats and vanilla.

Dissolve the bicarbonate of soda in 2 tablespoons of boiling water, then add to the butter mixture. Add the sifted flour and salt and mix well.

Roll into 24 small balls and place on the baking trays, allowing room for the biscuits to spread and flatten during cooking. Bake for 10–15 minutes, or until golden and cooked through. Remove from the oven and cool on the trays.

To make the ganache, put the chocolate in a heatproof bowl. Bring the cream to the boil in a small saucepan and pour over the chocolate. Leave to melt for 2 minutes, before mixing to a smooth, shiny ganache.

Add 150 g (5½ oz) of the ganache to the frosting, to make a chocolate frosting.

To assemble the biscuits, pipe a ring of chocolate frosting around the edge of half the biscuits. Place a spoonful of ganache in the centre and pop a lid on top.

The biscuits will keep in an airtight container in a cool dark place for up to 1 week.

RAZZLE DAZZLE

You could add some salty caramel (page 220) to the frosting, or a nip of liqueur, such as amaretto or Grand Marnier.

We only made this staple a few times in the opening days of the shop, and really must revisit this recipe more often. It's like listening to a country band at the local pub as the dulcet melancholic tones wash over you, and your soul, whilst inebriated, is soothed.

MAKES 1 LOAF

BANANA STICKY DATE LOAF

175 g (6 oz) butter
100 g (3½ oz) soft brown sugar
2 tablespoons honey
2 eggs
225 g (8 oz) plain (all-purpose) flour, sifted
1 teaspoon baking powder
3 ripe bananas, mashed
100 g (3½ oz) medjool dates, chopped
½ quantity of salty caramel (page 220)

Preheat the oven to 160°C (315°C/Gas 2-3). Line a 10 x 22 cm (4 x 8½ inch) loaf (bar) tin with baking paper.

Using electric beaters, beat the butter and sugar until pale and creamy. Add the honey, then add the eggs one at a time, scraping down the side of the bowl to make sure there are no stray buttery bits.

Fold in the sifted flour and baking powder, then add the banana and dates. Stir lightly, before depositing the batter into the loaf tin.

Bake for 1¼ hours, or until the loaf is golden brown and a skewer inserted into the middle comes out clean. Remove from the oven and leave in the tin.

Douse the loaf with the salty caramel, then leave to cool in the tin for 30 minutes, before placing on a serving plate.

The loaf will keep in an airtight container in a cool dark place for up to 1 week; the uncovered loaf can be frozen for up to 2 weeks.

'Smash cake' may sound like a weird idea: get a perfectly good cake, then take photos of your toddler making a real mess of it! It is usually done around the child's first birthday, with photos taken to mark the milestone. It is often the first time the child has eaten much cake and is allowed to do whatever they want with it — face-planting into it, putting icing in their hair, or knocking the whole thing over and then crawling through it.

MAKES TWO 18 CM (7 INCH), THREE-LAYER ROUND CAKES

VANILLA VANILLA SMASH CAKE

420 g (15 oz) butter
60 g (2¼ oz) liquid glucose
600 g (1 lb 5 oz) sugar
8 eggs
900 g (2 lb) plain (all-purpose) flour
40 g (1½ oz) baking powder
10 g (¼ oz) sea salt
400 ml (14 fl oz) water
1 teaspoon vanilla extract
creamy vanilla frosting (page 231); you'll need 2–3 quantities, depending on the final decoration you choose

Preheat the oven to 180°C (350°C/Gas 4). Line two 18 cm (7 inch) round cake tins with baking paper.

Using electric beaters, cream the butter, glucose and sugar until pale and creamy. Slowly add the eggs one at a time, beating well each time.

Sift the flour, baking powder and salt together into a bowl. Add the flour mixture to the butter mixture in batches, alternating with the water and vanilla. With each addition, beat until the ingredients are incorporated, but do not overmix.

Divide the batter between the cake tins and bake for 30 minutes, or until a skewer inserted into the middle of each cake comes out clean.

Leave to cool in the tins for 10 minutes, before turning out onto a wire rack to cool completely.

To assemble, cut each cake into three equal layers using a sharp knife or cake leveller. Place the first layer of each cake onto a cake board and pipe the frosting onto the cake. Place the next cake layer on top, and pipe the frosting over. Place the final cake layer on top and give each whole cake a fine coating of frosting; this is called 'dirty ice', and allows the crumbs to be trapped so they will not get into the final icing layer.

Once you have dirty-iced the cakes, allow the icing to firm up for 5 minutes in the fridge and you are ready to cover.

Get creative with a piping bag and nozzle and decorate the sides and top of the cake with any piped frosting decoration you like. Avoid using royal icing for the finish, as it is too firm for a child to smash. Think soft!

SMASHING GOOD TIPS

Vanilla is one of the best all-round cakes. You can turn it into something spectacular by adding a splash of lemon juice or a pinch of cinnamon to the batter, and filling the finished cake with jams, curds or caramel.

The cakes can be baked a day ahead; they'll be easier to layer and assemble if you do.

We would advise parents to avoid chocolate cake at all times, and red icing is probably best avoided too — we don't want those perfect birthday photos looking like something from a horror film!

Peanut sitting on a stainless steel bench... along comes a rolling pin and... uh oh, nutter butter: peanut butter cookies filled with peanut butter frosting, a spoonful of peanut butter and salty caramel sauce. Toot toot!

MAKES 12 BISCUITS

NUTTER BUTTERS

PEANUT COOKIES

125 g (4½ oz) butter
100 g (3½ oz) caster (superfine) sugar
100 g (3½ oz) soft brown sugar
1 egg, lightly beaten
225 g (8 oz) pastry flour, sifted
1 teaspoon baking powder
70 g (2½ oz) peanuts

Cream the butter and both sugars using electric beaters for about 5 minutes. Add the egg gradually, until well mixed and pale and creamy.

Add the sifted flour, baking powder and peanuts, being careful not to overmix. Roll the dough into two logs, about 5 cm (2 inches) in diameter. Cover with plastic wrap and freeze for about 1 hour, until firm; the dough can be made ahead and frozen for several weeks. Thaw until firm before cutting and baking.

Preheat the oven to 150°C (300°C/Gas 2). Line two baking trays with baking paper.

Cut the logs into 24 slices about 5 mm (¼ inch) thick, and space them apart on the baking trays, allowing room for a growth spurt in the oven. Bake for 10–15 minutes, or until an even golden brown. Remove from the oven and cool on the trays.

TO ASSEMBLE

50 g (1¾ oz) peanut butter, plus an extra 1 teaspoon for each biscuit
½ quantity of creamy vanilla frosting (page 231)
100 ml (3½ fl oz) salty caramel (page 220)

Add the 50 g (1¾ oz) of peanut butter to the frosting and mix thoroughly.

Pipe a ring of the peanut butter frosting around the edge of half the biscuits. Place 1 teaspoon peanut butter in the centre of each, top with a spoonful of salty caramel and add a second biscuit as a lid.

The biscuits will keep in an airtight container in a cool dark place for up to 1 week.

Macaron, macaroons... which do you prefer? You choose! Both are great in their own right — but anyone trying to put on his or her fancy pants will definitely go the macaron. Macarons have a light crispy shell, with a soft centre, and the traditional foot at the base. At our shop they get filled with jams, curds, flavoured butter creams or ganache.

MAKES 30 FILLED BISCUITS

MACARONS

8 egg whites
45 g (1½ oz) caster (superfine) sugar
1 teaspoon egg white powder
325 g (11½ oz) almond meal
500 g (1 lb 2 oz) icing (confectioners') sugar
food colouring (optional)
filling of your choice

Using an electric mixer, whisk the egg whites to stiff peaks. Add the sugar gradually, then the egg white powder, to make a nice firm meringue mixture.

Sift the almond meal and icing sugar through a fine sieve. Fold the meringue and the dry ingredients together; keep folding until the mixture falls back into itself without leaving a trace, ensuring all the dry ingredients are well incorporated. You want to keep the mixture on the firmer side, and not too runny; the longer you beat, the runnier it will get. At this stage you can add some colour to the mix if you want.

Put the mixture in a piping (icing) bag fitted with an 8 mm (3/8 inch) plain nozzle. Line two large baking trays with baking paper. Pipe bulbs about 4 cm (1½ inches) round onto the baking trays, leaving space between each.

Now tap the trays gently – this releases any excess air and flattens the macarons slightly. Allow to sit at room temperature for 30 minutes, or until a skin has formed.

Meanwhile, preheat the oven to 130°C (250°F/Gas 1). Bake the macarons for 10–15 minutes. To check if they are ready, lift one gently from the tray – if it comes clean away from the paper, the macarons are good to go.

Allow to cool, then match up pairs of macarons according to size and join with your favourite fillings (see below). We always double-fill the macarons using a butter cream or ganache to make a dam to hold a flavour-packed liquid filling – it's well worth a try.

FUNKY FLAVOURS

Add different flavoured food essences to some creamy vanilla frosting, and pair with a jam or sweet jazzed-up curd. Here are some of our favourite combos...

- **Pistachio frosting and strawberry jam**
- **Rose geranium frosting and raspberry jam**
- **Chocolate ganache (page 231) and passionfruit curd**
- **Caramel frosting (page 231) and caramel centre**
- **Jasmine frosting and lemon curd (page 221)**
- **Violet frosting and boysenberry jam**

MACARON MASTERY

The macarons will keep in an airtight container for 2 days once filled. Unfilled macarons can be frozen in an airtight container between sheets of baking paper for 3–4 weeks. They are easier to fill when frozen, and will take only about 10 minutes to thaw.

Macaroons are those moist, chewy, coconut-based meringue cookies that both of us made as apprentices, in what seems like the olden days! We'd make them in massive batches that had our arms aching by the time we'd finished piping them. But they're well worth the effort when you get a warm one just out of the oven.

MAKES 30 MACAROONS

MACAROONS

4 egg whites
125 g (4½ oz) caster (superfine) sugar
115 g (4 oz) desiccated (shredded) coconut
210 g (7½ oz) almond meal
30 raw almonds

Preheat the oven to 190°C (375°F/Gas 5). Line two large baking trays with baking paper.

Using electric beaters, whisk the egg whites to stiff peaks, then beat in half the sugar to make a firm meringue.

Fold in the coconut, almond meal and remaining sugar.

Put the mixture in a piping (icing) bag fitted with an 8 mm (⅜ inch) plain nozzle. Pipe small rosette shapes onto the lined baking trays, about 5 cm (2 inches) round, leaving space between each one.

Decorate each macaroon with a whole almond, then bake for 15 minutes. Remove from the oven and cool on the trays.

The biscuits will keep in an airtight container in a cool dark place for up to 2 weeks.

Bitter almonds can be a little hard to source, but are well worth seeking out. Add these amaretti to a tiramisu for a truly earth-shattering moment of foodie delight. Or dunk in strong coffee if a cup of tea just isn't going to get the job done.

MAKES 30 BISCUITS

AMARETTI

180 g (6 oz) almonds
45 g (1½ oz) bitter almonds
240 g (8½ oz) caster (superfine) sugar
3 egg whites
icing (confectioners') sugar, for dusting

Put all the almonds in a food processor with 180 g (6 oz) of the caster sugar. Mix until warm; this usually takes a few minutes.

Whisk the egg whites to stiff peaks. Now add the remaining 60 g (2¼ oz) caster sugar, whisking until you have a firm meringue.

Gently fold the almond mixture into the meringue, then place in a piping (icing) bag fitted with a 5 cm (2 inch) nozzle.

Line two baking trays with baking paper, then pipe small bulbs onto the baking trays. Dust with icing sugar and set aside for 30 minutes, or until the biscuits have formed a skin.

Meanwhile, preheat the oven to 200°C (400°C/Gas 6).

Pinch the biscuit mounds slightly to create a pattern, then bake for 10 minutes.

Turn the oven down to its lowest setting, place a wooden spoon in the door to hold it ajar and dry the biscuits out for an hour or so.

Pack in an airtight container, or wrap in wax paper for a truly authentic finish. The biscuits will keep in an airtight container in a cool dark place for up to 2 weeks.

Red velvet cake is a favourite of ours, resonating with stories of Grandma's recipe passed down through generations. Rich in colour and undeniable flavour, it also reminds us of the time we spent living in New York, ambling down Manhattan to Magnolia Bakery and lining up with the masses just to get some of those delicious cupcakes, smothered in creamy vanilla frosting... Happy times.

MAKES 24 CUPCAKES

RED VELVET CUPCAKES

185 g (6½ oz) butter
400 g (14 oz) sugar
3 eggs
430 g (15¼ oz) plain (all-purpose) flour
45 g (1½ oz) Dutch-processed cocoa powder
2 teaspoons bicarbonate of soda (baking soda)
a pinch of sea salt
375 ml (13 fl oz/1½ cups) buttermilk
2 teaspoons cider vinegar
2 teaspoons vanilla extract
1 tablespoon red food colouring
1 quantity of marshmallow (from the woffla recipe on page 99)

Preheat the oven to 180°C (350°C/Gas 4). Line two 12-hole 125 ml (4 fl oz/½ cup) muffin tins with paper cases.

Using electric beaters, cream the butter and sugar until pale and creamy. Slowly add the eggs one at a time, beating well each time.

Sift the flour, cocoa, bicarbonate of soda and sea salt together into a bowl.

Combine the buttermilk, vinegar, vanilla and food colouring in another bowl.

Add the flour mixture to the butter mixture in batches, alternating with the liquids. With each addition, beat until the ingredients are incorporated, but do not overmix.

Divide the batter among the muffin holes and bake for 20 minutes, or until a skewer inserted into the middle of a cupcake comes out clean.

Leave to cool in the tins for 10 minutes, before turning out onto a wire rack to cool completely.

Once cooled, smother the tops with the marshmallow.

The cupcakes will keep in an airtight container in a cool dark place for up 2 days; unfrosted cupcakes can be frozen for up to 2 weeks.

BRIAN

Sweet Envy
: THE WOFFLA
WOFFLA A WHOLE LOT OF WAFFLE GOING ON!! VOTE 1: THE WOFFLA A WHOLE LOT OF WAFFLE GOING ON!! VOTE 1: THE WOFFLA A WHOLE LOT
VOTE 1
Number the boxes from 1 to 10 in the order of your choice.
Number every box to make your vote count
MIT MAT
NUTTER BUTTER
MACAROON
WOFFLA
CANTUCCI
BADA BING
MARGATE
RO-VO
AMORETTI
HARVEY MILK

The good old Aussie 'Polly Waffle' — a marshmallow-filled, chocolate-covered wafer tube — has taken its turn at Sweet Envy and has become The Woffla: sheets of wafer brushed with local honey, stuffed with soft chewy marshmallow and dipped in chocolate. It all came about because an election was coming up, and the word in the shop was that there was a whole bunch of 'waffle' going on...

MAKES 12 BARS

THE WOFFLA

WAFER

50 g (1¾ oz) butter
50 g (1¾ oz) mildly fragrant honey (we use Tasmanian prickly box honey)
4 wafer sheets, about A4 size

Preheat the oven to 180°C (350°C/Gas 4). Line a baking tray with baking paper.

Melt the butter and honey in a small saucepan. Using a pastry brush, lightly brush the mixture over both sides of each wafer sheet.

Place the wafer sheets on the baking tray. Sit a sheet of baking paper on top, then another baking tray, so the wafers are sandwiched between the two trays.

Bake for 10–15 minutes, or until the wafer is golden brown and the honey has caramelised. Remove from the oven and cool on the tray.

Using a sharp serrated bread knife, cut the wafer into oblongs measuring about 3 x 10 cm (1¼ x 4 inches).

MARSHMALLOW

270 g (9½ oz) caster (superfine) sugar
180 g (6 oz) liquid glucose
15 g (½ oz) powdered gelatine

Put the sugar and glucose in a heavy-based saucepan with 70 ml (2¼ fl oz) of water. Bring to the boil and cook to the soft-ball stage (118°C/245°F on a sugar thermometer). Leave to cool to 100°C (212°F).

Put the gelatine in a heatproof bowl with 90 ml (3 fl oz) of cold water. After about 5 minutes, once the gelatine has soaked up all the water, place the bowl over a saucepan of hot water to melt the mixture briefly, then add it to the hot sugar syrup. Use hand-held electric beaters or a stand mixer with a whisk attachment to beat the marshmallow until light, fluffy and cool.

TO ASSEMBLE

300 g (10½ oz) dark chocolate, chopped
15 ml (½ fl oz) vegetable oil

Pipe the marshmallow onto half the wafers, then pop the wafer lids on top. Allow to firm for about 10 minutes.

Melt the chocolate in a heatproof bowl set over a saucepan of just simmering water, ensuring the base of the bowl doesn't touch the water. Add the oil and mix until fully emulsified.

One at a time, submerge the bottom half of each biscuit into the melted chocolate, so the marshmallow won't stick to everything. Drain off any excess chocolate before placing onto a lined tray to set.

These biscuits are best eaten the next day, as the marshmallow gets a nice chewy stickiness to it.

Here's our ode to the classic Australian Tim Tam biscuit, with loads of chocolate: chocolate cookies, creamy chocolate frosting and a chocolate ganache centre. Who wouldn't love it?

MAKES 12 BISCUITS

MIT MATS

CHOCOLATE BISCUITS

320 g (11¼ oz) pastry flour, sifted
80 g (2¾ oz) Dutch-processed cocoa powder, sifted
120 g (4¼ oz) icing (confectioners') sugar, sifted
240 g (8½ oz) butter
a pinch of sea salt
1 egg, lightly beaten

Rub together the sifted flour, cocoa, icing sugar, butter and salt to a fine crumb. Add the egg and mix as little as possible to bring the dough together. Wrap into 3–4 manageable portions and chill in the refrigerator for at least a couple of hours; the dough will easily keep for several days.

Preheat the oven to 180°C (350°C/Gas 4). Line two baking trays with baking paper. Roll out the dough to about 3 mm (⅛ inch) thick and cut into 24 oblongs, about 3 x 10 cm (1¼ x 4 inches) in size.

Place on the baking trays and bake for 10 minutes. It is difficult to tell if the dough is cooked, so gently try and move the biscuits on the tray; if they move easily, remove from the oven and cool on the tray.

TO ASSEMBLE

1 quantity of creamy vanilla frosting (page 231)
½ quantity of ganache (page 231)
450 g (1 lb) dark chocolate, chopped
50 ml (1½ fl oz) vegetable oil

Make the frosting and add 50 g (1¾ oz) of the ganache.

Pipe a strip of frosting along each edge of half the cooled biscuits, then pipe a strip of ganache through the centre and pop a lid on top. Leave to firm for about 30 minutes.

Melt the chocolate in a heatproof bowl set over a saucepan of just simmering water, ensuring the base of the bowl doesn't touch the water. Add the oil and mix until fully emulsified.

Submerge the biscuits in the melted chocolate one at a time, draining off any excess, before placing them on a lined tray to set. (Despite all the new-fangled gadgets that are available nowadays, we still use a table fork to do this, as anything a little better will more than likely end up in Matilda's play box, never to be seen again.)

The biscuits will keep in an airtight container in a cool dark place for up to 1 week.

The Carlton Club

The beautiful thing about tarts is that a tart shell can carry the most delicate of mousses and make it transportable; the shell itself is delicious, and with a little care in preparation will add a wonderful texture to the dish.

YOU TART!

This chapter title reminds me of those uncouth bogans we caught the school bus home with, waving their hands at the passing traffic and screaming out the window...

Frivolity aside, the beautiful thing about tarts is that a tart shell can carry the most delicate of mousses and make it transportable: the shell itself is delicious, and with a little care in preparation will add a wonderful texture to the dish.

Always, when making sweet tarts, brush them out with chocolate. Let's not get fancy and turn this into a huge process — just melt a bit of chocolate and smear it on the inside of the tart shell to seal the pastry and stop moisture migration (aka soggy tarts). We've all been there, when we've purchased a tart and the pastry feels like a soggy biscuit.

When storing tarts, keep them in an airtight container to stop them absorbing moisture and odours from the atmosphere. Some of the tarts in this chapter have quite a few components, so protecting all your hard work by using the right type of container is well worth it.

The secret to our tarts is to prepare some of the bits a few days ahead. The best pastry chefs in the world may well not be the most technically advanced — just better at logistics. I will give you an example: if we were to make the Alfonso Pompelmousse tart on page 121, we'd start making the mango mousse and coconut mousse two days before, the following day we'd make the jelly and tart shells, then we'd serve the tart on the third day. It is so much easier to spread your workload.

We have a small team (just Teena and me!), so it's easier to keep on top of things by preparing a few little bits every day. While a small team can be dynamic, we bore easily with monotony, so this also keeps life interesting, no two days alike.

If you're having a dinner party, preparing most of the tart ahead will also leave you free to look after that expensive and all-important main-course protein. And of course give you a bit more time to settle back and relax!

Shaker lemon pie is one of our absolute favourites. We have an old fella named Laurrie who drops off crackingly good Meyer lemons to us, which work fabulously well in this recipe because of their softer skin. You really need to start this recipe the day before, and bake just before serving, as it is irresistibly good warm!

MAKES SIX 10 CM (4 INCH) PIES, OR ONE 20 CM (8 INCH) PIE

SHAKE & BAKE

4 lemons
250 g (9 oz) caster (superfine) sugar, plus extra for sprinkling
4 eggs
pinch of sea salt
1 quantity of puff pastry (page 227)
1 egg, lightly beaten

Cut the lemons in half across the middle. Remove the seeds and place the lemons in the freezer for half an hour. Slice as thinly possible, using a mandoline if you have one, and place in a stainless steel bowl. Add the sugar, cover and leave overnight.

The next day, lightly whisk the eggs with the salt. Now add the lemon slices – juice, peel and all.

Have a 20–25 cm (8–10 inch) tart mould or pie dish at the ready, or six 10 cm (4 inch) ones.

Roll out the pastry to about 3 mm (1/8 inch) thick and line whichever tart moulds or pie dishes you decide to use. Lightly press the pastry into the mould or moulds, making sure to get right into the corners.

Fill the pie shell or shells with the lemon mixture. Top with a pastry lid and crimp the edges. Leave to rest in the fridge for 1 hour.

Preheat the oven to 200°C (400°F/Gas 6).

Brush the top of the pie or pies with beaten egg and sprinkle with extra sugar. Bake for about 25 minutes for small pies, and 35–40 minutes for a large pie.

If you can resist, cool slightly before eating, but I doubt you'll be able to!

BACK
OVEN TOP
OVEN BOTTOM
MEDIUM
HIGH
LOW
OFF

There's not much to say about this one. Really it's just an adult version of caramel slice or millionaire's slice. You don't even need a recipe — just fill some tart shells with salty caramel and top with ganache. Always make extra, as I am sure in the near future these tarts will replace the need for money.

MAKES ONE 20–25 CM (8–10 INCH) TART, OR A DOZEN 10 CM (4 INCH) TARTS

CHOCOLATE SALTY CARAMEL TARTS

1 quantity of chocolate sweet pastry (page 225)
1 handful of chopped dark chocolate, melted
1 quantity of salty caramel (page 220)
½ quantity of ganache (page 231)

Preheat the oven to 170°C (325°F/Gas 3). Have a 20–25 cm (8–10 inch) tart mould or pie dish at the ready, or twelve 10 cm (4 inch) ones.

Roll out the pastry to about 3 mm (⅛ inch) thick, then cut out a disc or discs slightly bigger than your tart mould or moulds. Lightly press the pastry in, making sure to get right into the corners. Trim the edges with the back of a knife and place on a baking tray.

Line the pastry with baking paper (or flatten a paper case into each one). Fill with baking beads or raw rice, then bake for 10–12 minutes for small pies, or 15–20 minutes for a large pie, until the pastry is cooked through.

Remove from the oven and carefully lift out the paper and beads. Leave to cool.

Using a pastry brush, coat the inside of the cooled tart shell or shells with a thin layer of chocolate, to stop moisture migration.

Store in an airtight container until required; the tart shells will keep for a day or so.

Fill the tart shells halfway with salty caramel and top with the ganache.

Allow to set for about 30 minutes and then devour straight away, or chill in the fridge for up to 2 days.

This idea is in fact one I've stolen from chef Paul Foreman, who was tenured at Marque IV in Hobart while I was waiting for my visa to come through for New York. I forgot to get the recipe from him so I had to make it up from memory. However it's an absolute cracker, and gives the old custard tart some hipness and zing.

MAKES ONE 30 CM (12 INCH) TART

GIN & LIME TART

BASE

1½ quantities of sweet pastry (page 225)
1 egg, lightly beaten

Preheat the oven to 170°C (325°F/Gas 3). Have a 30 cm (12 inch) tart mould or pie dish at the ready.

Roll out the pastry to about 3 mm (⅛ inch) thick, then cut out a disc slightly bigger than your tart mould. Lightly press the pastry into the mould, making sure to get right into the corners. Trim the edge with the back of a knife and place on a baking tray.

Line the pastry shell with baking paper. Fill with baking beads or raw rice and bake for 15–20 minutes, or until the pastry is cooked through.

Remove from the oven and carefully lift out the paper and beads.

Brush the hot tart shell with the beaten egg, as this will seal any misdemeanours, hopefully making the tart custard-tight, and relieving the house of smoke infestation and the irrational bleating of your smoke detector.

Prepare the custard while the tart shell is still warm.

WASTE NOT
While you are in your cooking motions, use the left-over egg whites from the custard to make a batch of macarons (page 93) or macaroons (page 94).

GIN & LIME CUSTARD

1 vanilla bean, cut in half lengthways, seeds scraped
150 ml (5 fl oz) gin
grated zest and juice of 4 limes
500 ml (17 fl oz/2 cups) thin (pouring) cream
8 egg yolks
250 g (9 oz) caster (superfine) sugar
your choice of cream, to serve

Turn the oven down to 130°C (250°F/Gas 1).

Put the vanilla seeds, gin, lime zest, lime juice and cream into a saucepan and bring to just below the boil (80°C/176°F on a sugar thermometer).

Lightly whisk the egg yolks and sugar until just combined, then add a little of the warmed cream. Now pour all the mixture back into the saucepan and cook for 5 minutes, or until the mixture coats the back of a spoon (83°C/181°F on a sugar thermometer).

Pour the custard into the warm tart shell and bake for 20 minutes, or until the custard has set.

Leave the tart to cool, then cool in the fridge for at least 30 minutes before attempting to slice into large portions.

Serve with cream of any description – clotted, thick (double) cream or softly whipped cream. Best enjoyed within 1–2 days.

Quince has to be one of our favourite fruits. Once poached and sealed in an airtight container, with a round of baking paper on top, it will last well for several months in the fridge. Here it crowns one of the British classics: treacle tart. Serve with lashings of cream or crème fraîche on a cool winter's day.

MAKES ONE 20 CM (8 INCH) TART

QUINTRECALICIOUS

SLOW-COOKED QUINCE

5 quinces
200 g (7 oz) caster (superfine) sugar

Peel and quarter the quinces, removing the cores. Put the cores and peelings onto a piece of muslin (cheesecloth) and tie up with kitchen string.

Put the sugar and 500 ml (17 fl oz/2 cups) of water in a large heavy-based saucepan. Bring to the boil, then add the quince and the muslin parcel. Cover with a round of baking paper and bring to a slow simmer. Cook, without the lid on, for 6 hours, or until the quince turns a deep, dark red.

Transfer the quince and syrup to an airtight container, cover with a round of baking paper, seal the lid and keep until required. The quince will keep in the fridge for 3–6 months.

TREACLE TART

1 quantity of sweet pastry (page 225)
85 g (3 oz) brioche crumbs
60 g (2¼ oz) almond meal
300 g (10½ oz) golden syrup or mild honey
150 ml (5 fl oz) thin (pouring) cream
1 egg
1 handful of almonds, for scattering

Preheat the oven to 170°C (325°F/Gas 3). Have a 20 cm (8 inch) tart mould or pie dish at the ready.

Roll out the pastry to about 3 mm (⅛ inch) thick, then cut out a disc slightly bigger than your tart mould. Lightly press the pastry into the mould, making sure to get right into the corners. Trim the edge with the back of a knife and place on a baking tray.

Line the pastry shell with baking paper. Fill with baking beads or raw rice and bake for 15–20 minutes, or until the pastry is cooked through.

Remove from the oven and carefully lift out the paper and beans.

While the tart shell is cooling, put the brioche crumbs and almond meal in a food processor and blitz until combined. Warm the golden syrup and cream in a small saucepan and add to the food processor. Add the egg and mix until smooth. Pour into the tart shell.

Add as much of the quince as you like – we recommend 12–15 pieces, so you have some left over to go with your yoghurt and muesli for breakfast.

Sprinkle with the almonds and bake for 25–30 minutes, or until golden brown all over. Check that the base of your tart is cooked – this is a heavy mixture, so sometimes you may need to cook it a little longer.

Best enjoyed within 1–2 days.

Sydney's Bourke Street Bakery is famous for its brûlée tarts. We went there, had 'em, loved 'em, stole 'em. Here's the version we make for the Saturday onslaught in Hobart. The Geeveston Fanny is an apple variety grown locally in Tassie. Truth be known it is not the world's best cooking apple — but the name is evocative.

MAKES SIX 10 CM (4 INCH) TARTS

GEEVESTON FANNY

BASE

½ quantity of sweet pastry (page 225)
1 handful of chopped dark chocolate, melted

Preheat the oven to 170°C (325°F/Gas 3). Have six 10 cm (4 inch) tart moulds or pie dishes at the ready.

Roll out the pastry to about 3 mm (⅛ inch) thick. Cut out six pastry discs, slightly bigger than your tart moulds. Lightly press the pastry into the moulds, making sure to get right into the corners. Trim the edges with the back of a knife and place on a baking tray.

Line the pastry shells with baking paper (or flatten a paper case into each one). Fill with baking beads or raw rice, then bake for 10–12 minutes, or until the pastry is cooked through.

Remove from the oven and carefully lift out the paper and beads. Leave to cool.

Using a pastry brush, coat the inside of the cooled tart shells with a thin layer of chocolate, to stop moisture migration.

Store in an airtight container until required; the tart shells will keep for a day or so.

WHAT A BLAST
When topping the brûlée, we have always found that a few layers of sugar holds up a lot longer than a single layer, and also gives you a much better 'crack' when breaking into the creamy goodness underneath.

APPLE CRÈME

90 g (3¼ oz) apple purée
300 ml (10½ fl oz) thin (pouring) cream
½ vanilla bean, cut in half lengthways, seeds scraped
6 egg yolks
30 g (1 oz) caster (superfine) sugar

Preheat the oven to 90°C (195°F/Gas ½). Warm the apple purée, cream and vanilla seeds in a saucepan, then remove from the heat. Leave to infuse for 15 minutes.

Lightly whisk the egg yolks and sugar, then pour in the cream mixture and stir to combine.

Pass the mixture through a fine sieve, into a 15–20 cm (6–8 inch) baking dish.

Bake for 30 minutes, or until the custard has set.

TO ASSEMBLE

raw (demerara) sugar, for sprinkling

Allow the custard to cool, then plaster the tart shells full to the brim with the mix.

Sprinkle the top with raw sugar, then use a kitchen blowtorch (or flame thrower, depending on what Grandad keeps in the shed!) to blast the top until caramelised.

These tarts are best enjoyed same day.

This English classic is normally made by boiling condensed milk in the tin until it turns into a thick caramel. We find the caramel a little cloyingly sweet, so we use our banana jam to lessen the sweetness and up the pleasure.

MAKES ONE 20–25 CM (8–10 INCH) TART, OR A DOZEN 10 CM (4 INCH) TARTS

BANOFFEE

BASE

1 quantity of chocolate sweet pastry (page 225)
1 handful of chopped dark chocolate, melted

Preheat the oven to 170°C (325°F/Gas 3). Have a 20–25 cm (8–10 inch) tart mould or pie dish at the ready, or twelve 10 cm (4 inch) ones.

Roll out the pastry to about 3 mm (⅛ inch) thick, then cut out a disc or discs slightly bigger than your tart mould or moulds. Lightly press the pastry in, making sure to get right into the corners. Trim the edges with the back of a knife and place on a baking tray.

Line the pastry with baking paper (or flatten a paper case into each one). Fill with baking beads or raw rice, then bake for 10–12 minutes for small pies, or 15–20 minutes for a large pie, until the pastry is cooked through.

Remove from the oven and carefully lift out the paper and beads. Leave to cool.

Using a pastry brush, coat the inside of each cooled tart shell with a thin layer of chocolate, to stop moisture migration.

Store in an airtight container until required; the tart shells will keep for a day or so.

MILK CHOCOLATE TRUFFLE

200 g (7 oz) milk chocolate, chopped
100 ml (3½ fl oz) thin (pouring) cream
150 ml (5 fl oz) lightly whipped cream

Put the chocolate in a heatproof bowl and set aside.

Bring the cream to the boil, then pour over the chocolate and whisk until smooth and emulsified. Lightly fold in the whipped cream.

TO ASSEMBLE

1 quantity of banana jam (page 222)
½ quantity of ganache (page 231)

Smear each tart shell with a generous layer of banana jam. Pipe the chocolate truffle mixture into each tart shell. Spoon lashings of ganache over the top.

Eat straight away, or chill in the fridge for up to 2 days.

Ahhh, Neenish tart! Quintessentially Australian, it evokes memories of my mum's kitchen, laden with goodies. Mum always — at least in *my* memory — added a dash of rum from Dad's booze cupboard when making these tarts. Although their true origins are unknown, a *Sydney Morning Herald* columnist attributes them to Mrs Ruby Neenish, so Mrs Ruby is the name we sell these beauties under.

MAKES SIX 10 CM (4 INCH) TARTS

MRS RUBY

BASE

½ quantity of sweet pastry (page 225)
1 handful of chopped dark chocolate, melted

Preheat the oven to 170°C (325°F/Gas 3). Have six 10 cm (4 inch) tart moulds or pie dishes at the ready.

Roll out the pastry to about 3 mm (⅛ inch) thick. Cut out six pastry discs, slightly bigger than your tart moulds. Lightly press the pastry into the moulds, making sure to get right into the corners. Trim the edges with the back of a knife and place on a baking tray.

Line the pastry shells with baking paper, or flatten a paper case into each one. Fill with baking beads or raw rice, then bake for 10–12 minutes, or until the pastry is cooked through. Remove from the oven and carefully lift out the paper and beads. Leave to cool.

Using a pastry brush, coat the inside of the cooled tart shells with a thin layer of chocolate, to stop moisture migration.

Store in an airtight container until required; the tart shells will keep for a day or two.

RUM RAISINS

200 g (7 oz) raisins
100 ml (3½ fl oz) decent rum

Soak the raisins in the rum for a few hours, or until good and boozy; overnight is ideal.

RUM CREAM

8 g (⅙ oz) gelatine sheets
50 ml (1½ fl oz) decent rum
400 ml (14 fl oz) thin (pouring) cream, whipped to medium peaks

Soak the gelatine in cold water for 5 minutes. Drain and squeeze out the excess liquid. Warm the rum, then add the gelatine and stir to dissolve. Fold the mixture into the whipped cream.

WATER ICING

200 g (7 oz) icing (confectioners') sugar
a pinch of Dutch-processed cocoa powder

Boil 75 ml (2¼ fl oz) of water, then mix in the icing sugar until smooth. Divide the icing into two equal portions and mix the cocoa through one portion.

TO ASSEMBLE

Drain the raisins. Spoon some raisins into the bottom of each tart shell as a cheeky surprise for Grandma, then smother the rum cream into the tart shells, right to the very brim.

Using a palette knife, cover half the tart with a very thin layer of white icing, then cover the other half with the chocolate icing. Allow the icing to set, then enjoy. These tarts are best enjoyed the day they are assembled.

Our version of a much-loved classic. We make ours in individual portions. Start these a day ahead, as the lemon curd needs to set in the fridge overnight before using. Also make the lemon cakes the day before, so they will be less crumbly to cut.

MAKES 6

LEMON MERINGUE

BASE

½ quantity of sweet pastry (page 225)

Preheat the oven to 180°C (350°F/Gas 4). Line a baking tray with baking paper. Roll out the pastry to about 4 mm (⅙ inch) thick. Cut out six 9 cm (3½ inch) discs. Place on the baking tray and bake for 10 minutes, or until golden.

LEMON CAKES

110 g (3¾ oz) butter
grated zest of 1 lemon
115 g (4 oz) caster (superfine) sugar
2 eggs
120 g (4¼ oz) plain (all-purpose) flour
1 teaspoon baking powder

Preheat the oven to 180°C (350°F/Gas 4). Line six holes of a 125 ml (½ cup) muffin tin with paper cases.

Using an electric mixer, beat the butter, lemon zest and sugar until pale and creamy. Add the eggs one at a time and continue to beat until smooth. Fold in the flour and baking powder.

Spoon the batter into the paper cases; we like to pipe the mixture into the cases as this usually gives a nice even top.

Bake for 12 minutes, or until a skewer inserted into the middle comes out clean. Remove and leave to cool in the tin for 10 minutes, then turn out, remove the paper cases and set aside.

ITALIAN MERINGUE

200 g (7 oz) caster (superfine) sugar
130 g (4½ oz) egg whites

Put the sugar in a saucepan with 65 ml (2 fl oz) of water. Bring to the boil and cook to the soft-ball stage (118°C/245°F on a sugar thermometer).

Using an electric mixer, whisk the egg whites to stiff peaks, then very carefully pour the sugar syrup down the side of the bowl. Whisk for a further 10 minutes, or until cool.

TO ASSEMBLE

½ quantity of lemon curd (page 221)

We use a cake wheel to make assembling these easier, but a plate placed on top of an upturned bowl seems to work well at home.

Use a cookie cutter to cut out the centre of each lemon cake, so you are left with a ring about 1 cm (½ inch) wide (the cut-out centres will sustain you during the following steps).

Place a ring of cake on top of a pastry disc and fill the hole with lemon curd. Cover the entire cake with meringue and pull out the kitchen blowtorch to make it a pretty colour.

These will sit quite happily for several hours before serving.

A tribute to New York pastry chef Christina Tosi, and to my favourite TV serial killer. For some extra crunch you can sprinkle the tarts with some CFC (page 224). The sesame brittle is also optional, but as with a few of the other elements can be made well ahead.

MAKES SIX 10 CM (4 INCH) TARTS

DEXTER

SESAME BRITTLE (OPTIONAL)

100 g (3½ oz) caster (superfine) sugar
a pinch of bicarbonate of soda (baking soda)
50 g (1¾ oz) sesame seeds

Have two sheets of baking paper ready.

Make a dry caramel by placing the sugar in a heavy-based frying pan over medium heat; cook, stirring occasionally, until the sugar has dissolved. Increase the heat and cook for 4–5 minutes, stirring occasionally at the beginning, but more vigorously towards the end, until the sugar turns a dark amber colour.

Once you have your desired colour, add the bicarbonate of soda, then quickly add the sesame seeds, before pouring the mixture onto one of the sheets of baking paper. Place the other sheet on top. Roll the caramel until thin, using a rolling pin. Set the brittle aside to harden.

Store in an airtight container for up to 1 week. Break into small shards to decorate.

TART SHELLS

½ quantity of sweet pastry (page 225)
1 handful of chopped dark chocolate, melted

Preheat the oven to 170°C (325°F/Gas 3). Have six 10 cm (4 inch) tart moulds or pie dishes at the ready.

Roll out the pastry to about 3 mm (⅛ inch) thick. Cut out six pastry discs, slightly bigger than your tart moulds. Lightly press the pastry into the moulds, making sure to get right into the corners. Trim the edges with the back of a knife and place on a baking tray.

Line the pastry shells with baking paper (or flatten a paper case into each one). Fill with baking beads or raw rice, then bake for 10–12 minutes, or until the pastry is cooked.

Remove from the oven and carefully lift out the paper and beads. Leave to cool.

Using a pastry brush, coat the inside of the cooled tart shells with a thin layer of chocolate, to stop moisture migration.

Store in an airtight container until required; the tart shells will keep for a day or so.

»

»

SERIAL MILK MOUSSE

4 g (1/9 oz) gelatine sheets
20 g (3/4 oz) CFC (page 224) or lightly roasted cornflakes
100 ml (3½ fl oz) milk
4 egg yolks
20 g (3/4 oz) caster (superfine) sugar
a pinch of sea salt
120 ml (4 fl oz) thin (pouring) cream

Soak the gelatine in a bowl of cold water for 5 minutes. Drain and squeeze out the excess liquid.

Put the CFC or cornflakes in a spice grinder and whiz to a powder.

Warm the milk, remove from the heat and add the CFC or cornflakes. Add a little of the warmed milk to the egg yolks with the sugar and salt, then add back to the milk in the pan and cook until the mixture coats the back of a spoon (83°C/181°F on a sugar thermometer).

While the mixture is still warm, stir in the gelatine to dissolve. Chill the mixture slightly.

Lightly whip the cream until soft peaks form, then gently fold into the chilled mixture.

Lightly grease six individual pudding moulds that are a bit smaller in diameter than the tart shells, so the mousse will sit inside the tarts.

Divide the mousse mixture among the moulds and chill for several hours, or until set.

If not using same day, the mousse can be covered and frozen in the moulds for up to 3 months; simply dip in hot water to unmould.

RHUBARB PURÉE

2 rhubarb stalks, finely sliced
splash of white wine
sprinkle of sugar

Put the rhubarb into a hot saucepan with the wine and sugar. Cook over medium heat for 4–5 minutes, or until the rhubarb is just tender, but leaving some texture in the purée. Set aside to cool.

CARDAMOM GLAZE

100 ml (3½ fl oz) thin (pouring) cream
5 cardamom pods
100 g (3½ oz) best-quality milk chocolate

Bring the cream and cardamom pods to the boil, then remove from the heat and set aside to infuse for about 15 minutes.

Put the chocolate in a heatproof bowl.

Bring the cream back to the boil, then strain it over the chocolate. Stir until the chocolate melts and you have a smooth glossy glaze for the mousse.

TO ASSEMBLE

Take the tart shells and put a lashing of the rhubarb purée in the bottom. Dip each mousse mould into hot water to unmould, then ease a mousse into each tart.

Spoon some cardamom glaze over the top so it slightly runs over the edge. Garnish with a little sesame brittle, if desired.

These tarts are best enjoyed the same day.

Yes, there are typos in the French spelling of 'grapefruit'... but I love raising the ire of the students from the French school up the road with our blatant ignorance. What originally was a simple spelling mistake has become the source of such great pleasure that I am sure it will never change.

MAKES SIX 10 CM (4 INCH) TARTS

ALFONSO POMPELMOUSSE

PINK GRAPEFRUIT JELLY

5 g (1/8 oz) gelatine sheets
1 pink grapefruit
1 tablespoon mango purée
100 ml (3½ fl oz) pink grapefruit juice
2 teaspoons caster (superfine) sugar

Soak the gelatine in a bowl of cold water for 5 minutes. Drain and squeeze out the excess liquid.

Meanwhile, finely grate the zest from the grapefruit. Cut a slice off the base of the grapefruit so it sits flat, then carefully slice off the skin and bitter white pith. Remove the fruit segments by slicing down in between each membrane. Dice the segments.

Warm the mango purée in a small saucepan. Add the gelatine and stir to dissolve, then add the grapefruit juice, sugar and grapefruit zest and segments.

Set the jelly in a container in the fridge for about 1 hour; the jelly can be made up to 1 week ahead.

MANGO MOUSSE

9 g (¼ oz) gelatine sheets
130 g (4½ oz) mango purée
3 egg yolks
60 g (2¼ oz) caster (superfine) sugar
130 g (4½ oz) lightly whipped cream

Soak the gelatine in cold water for 5 minutes. Drain and squeeze out the excess liquid.

Warm the mango purée in a small saucepan. Add the gelatine and stir to dissolve.

Make a sabayon by putting the egg yolks and sugar in a heatproof bowl over a pan of barely simmering water, ensuring the base of the bowl does not touch the water. Using electric beaters, whisk for about 5 minutes, or until the mixture has thickened and has the consistency of softly whipped cream.

Fold the lightly whipped cream into the mango mixture, followed by the sabayon. Pour into a greased 20 cm (8 inch) triangle terrine mould, approximately 5 cm (2 inches) deep.

Set in the freezer for about 1 hour; the mousse can be made up to 2 days ahead.

»

»

COCONUT & WHITE CHOCOLATE MOUSSE

100 ml (3½ fl oz) coconut cream
20 g (¾ oz) caster (superfine) sugar
2 teaspoons plain (all-purpose) flour
1 egg yolk
100 g (3½ oz) white chocolate
100 ml (3½ fl oz) thin (pouring) cream

Put the coconut cream in a saucepan and bring to the boil.

Combine the sugar, flour and egg yolk, then add to the pan and whisk until smooth. Cook, stirring occasionally, for about 4 minutes, until there is no taste of raw flour left. Take off the heat, add the chocolate and stir until smooth and emulsified.

Whisk the cream to soft peaks, then gently fold through the custard mixture. Pour into a container and set in the fridge for about 1 hour; the mousse can be made up to 2 days ahead.

TART SHELLS

½ quantity of sweet pastry (page 225)
1 handful of chopped dark chocolate, melted

Preheat the oven to 170°C (325°F/Gas 3). Have six 10 cm (4 inch) tart moulds or pie dishes at the ready.

Roll out the pastry to about 3 mm (⅛ inch) thick. Cut out six pastry discs, slightly bigger than your tart moulds. Lightly press the pastry into the moulds, making sure to get right into the corners. Trim the edges with the back of a knife and place on a baking tray.

Line the pastry shells with baking paper (or flatten a paper case into each one). Fill with baking beads or raw rice, then bake for 10–12 minutes, or until the pastry is cooked.

Remove from the oven and carefully lift out the paper and beads. Leave to cool.

Using a pastry brush, coat the inside of the cooled tart shells with a thin layer of chocolate, to stop moisture migration.

Store in an airtight container until required; the tart shells will keep for a day or so.

TO ASSEMBLE

dehydrated raspberries (optional)

Spoon the coconut mousse into the tart shells until it reaches the top edge. Top with a thin layer of the grapefruit jelly, enough to cover the coconut mousse.

Remove the mango mousse from the freezer and unmould by dipping the base into some hot water. Take a decent slice of the mango mousse and rest atop the jelly.

If you happen to have any kicking about, scatter with some dehydrated raspberries, for added texture and colour. These tarts are best enjoyed the same day.

CAKEATORIUM

These cakes are quite time-consuming, so we suggest making them over a few days: bake the cake one day, fill and finish it another day, then add the final touches to make it pop. Mother (pages 216–241) is on hand to help guide you.

Teena is the cake boss and runs the rather serious side of the business, dealing with all the brides-to-be (and their mothers!) and birthday and special-event cake orders. Thank god, as this leaves me to run around like a lark.

Teena's curious addiction started before we left for London. We photographed loads of Teena's cakes in various configurations on the floor and table of her parents' house, but on arriving in London, we found most of the cake decorating shops were based outside the city — too far to commute — while those in the central zones weren't really interested in an Aussie upstart with a small portfolio.

Instead, Teena spent her split shifts at an obligatory Michelin-starred restaurant, The Greenhouse, sitting in London's Green Park reading cake magazines and pining for a cake opportunity.

After working for a while for Angela Hartnett at the Connaught hotel, luck intervened, when 'big Ange' asked me to make a cake for the Chelsea Football Club. I was at a loss until Teena pointed out there was a cake shop close by in Putney. So off we went and gathered our supplies. As we left the cake shop, Teena ventured to ask if she could bring in her portfolio. The manager agreed, Teena returned, and finally found herself where she wanted to be.

English wedding cakes are full-on, no expense spared, and with the small team and a fantastic chemistry, fabulous cakes ensued.

There came a time to head home as our visas were up. We were back in Hobart, when an email arrived with the offer of a restaurant opening in New York.

Teena has always had an obsession with flowers, and the restaurant in New York was decorated by Jane Packer, one of the world's most influential florists. Through pure dumb luck and a little bluff we wrangled Teena into Jane Packer's shop, where she got to make some truly beautiful floral arrangements in an intense training extravaganza.

When we finally returned to Hobart, Teena's love affair continued. Her knowledge of flowers and her contacts have been essential to embellishing our cakes in modern designs.

The fabulous thing about Teena's cakes is that the more intricate the design, the more likely she is to take an order on!

We took an order for one of the doll cakes on display in the shop window, and had a good giggle when we noticed that the order, from a lovely lass named Betty, was actually for a 'Dolly Pardon' cake, instead of the usual Dolly Varden cake. So, naturally we thought it necessary to create this cake especially for Betty!

SERVES 25–30

DOLLY PARDON

FOR THE CAKE

- 17.5 cm (7 inch) round cake
- 20 cm (8 inch) round cake
- filling of choice, such as creamy vanilla frosting (page 231) or ganache (page 231); for quantities see page 241
- sugar paste (rolled fondant), in colours of your choice, for covering the base board and dress; for quantities see page 239

YOU WILL ALSO NEED

- 30 cm (12 inch) round base board
- 20 cm (8 inch) round cake board
- 1 beautiful doll of your choice
- ribbon

First, cover your base board with sugar paste (see page 233). Finish with ribbon trim, then set the board to one side until needed.

Cut each cake horizontally into three equal layers. Reassemble the layers, then stack the smaller cake on top of the larger one.

Using a sharp knife, start to carve away the edges, from top to bottom, into the shape of a ballooning ballroom dress, turning the cake regularly to keep a nice, even edge, until you have a dress shape you are happy with. Make sure you keep the base at 20 cm (8 inch); the top of the cake needs to be a suitable waist size for your chosen doll. You can make the dress look as full and rounded as you like at this stage.

Separate the cake layers on the bench. Cut out a disc in the centre of each layer, using a 3–4 cm (1¼ inch–1½ inch) cutter. Place the bottom layer on the cake board. Layer with your choice of filling up to the smallest layer, then dirty-ice (see page 234). Leave to set for 10 minutes.

Wrap the doll's legs in plastic wrap. Insert the doll, legs and all, into the centre of the cake.

FOR THE DRESS

Cover the whole cake with a layer of sugar paste, about 5 mm (¼ inch) thick (see page 234), to form the base of your dress. To do this, roll out a long strip of sugar paste, the height of your cake and about 60 cm (24 inches) long, then wrap it around the cake, starting at the back and overlapping at the end.

Gently smooth the sugar paste upwards, to remove any pleats at the top edge into the waist area. Trim with a sharp knife and smooth with your hand to get a nice seam. To create the dress layers, roll out another long strip of sugar paste in a different colour, the height of your cake and about 40 cm (16 inches) long. Wrap it around the cake, starting to one side at the front, and joining at the waist, but not the base, to give it that 'sweeping movement' look. Place the cake on the covered base board.

TO FINISH

Decorate the dress in any colour and design you wish. We've chosen a blossom and pearl design that starts at the waist and wraps all the way around the dress, with a few extra frilly bits towards the top of the dress.

Dressing a cake with fresh flowers can bring it to life instantly. Using the blocking method, you can create height and the illusion that the cake is suspended on a bed of flowers. This is a versatile design that can be used with many different flowers and foliage — even flowers to match a bridal bouquet. Roses are particularly effective, as there are so many varieties and colours available. Don't underestimate how many flowers you may need: the exact number will depend on their actual size.

SERVES 100–120

CLASSIC ELEGANCE WITH ROSES

FOR THE CAKE

- 15 cm (6 inch) round cake
- 20 cm (8 inch) round cake
- 25 cm (10 inch) round cake
- 30 cm (12 inch) round cake
- filling of choice, such as creamy vanilla frosting (page 231) or ganache (page 231); for quantities see page 241
- sugar paste (rolled fondant), for covering the base board and cakes; for quantities see page 239
- marzipan or almond sugar paste (rolled fondant), for covering the cakes; for quantities see page 239
- 1 quantity of royal icing (page 230)

YOU WILL ALSO NEED

- 37.5 cm (15 inch) round base board
- 15 cm (6 inch) round cake board
- 20 cm (8 inch) round cake board
- 25 cm (10 inch) round cake board
- 30 cm (12 inch) round cake board
- 10 cm (4 inch) foam block, about 7.5 cm (3 inches) high
- 15 cm (6 inch) foam block, about 7.5 cm (3 inches) high
- 20 cm (8 inch) foam block, about 7.5 cm (3 inches) high
- dowels
- 50–60 fresh roses or other flowers (make sure they have stems)
- 22-gauge florist's wire
- small florist's oasis dome
- ribbon

First, cover your base board with sugar paste (see page 233). Finish with ribbon trim, then set the board to one side until needed.

Cut each cake horizontally into three equal layers, then place the bottom third of each cake on a cake board of the same size. Layer each cake with your choice of filling, then dirty-ice (see page 234).

You should now have four filled and dirty-iced cake tiers, each with three layers.

Cover each tier with a layer of marzipan or almond sugar paste, about 3 mm (1/8 inch) thick (see page 234). Leave the cakes out on the bench overnight to set the sugar paste and make it more manageable.

The next day, cover each tier with another layer of plain sugar paste, about 5 mm (1/4 inch) thick. Finish with ribbon trim around the base of each cake tier.

At this stage we've used royal icing in a piping (icing) bag fitted with a small tip to create a more detailed effect by piping small balls in a random pattern around the sides of the cake.

Using the blocking method (see page 237), place the largest cake onto the covered base board. Position the 20 cm (8 inch) foam block in the centre and hold in place with royal icing.

»

»

Place the 15 cm (6 inch) foam block in the centre of the second-largest cake and secure with royal icing. Repeat with the remaining foam block and the 20 cm (8 inch) cake.

Using dowels for support around the foam blocks, and working from largest cake to smallest, stack the cake tiers centrally on top of each other, topping each foam block with more royal icing to hold it in place.

PREPARING THE FLOWERS

Trim each flower, leaving about 2 cm (¾ inch) of the stem intact.

Cut each piece of florist's wire into four lengths. Insert a length of florist's wire into the base of each flower (this will help secure the flowers to the foam blocks).

Insert the wired end of each flower into the foam blocks, working your way around each tier.

When you get to the top tier, make a small posy with approximately 10 flowers. Using the florist's oasis dome, start inserting the flowers around the base and then fill in the gap on top. You should end up with a nice dome-shaped posy to sit atop your tiers of splendour.

FLORAL FLAIR
When using a mixture of different flowers (similar to a bridal bouquet), you can save time by using one piece of wire for several flowers and binding them together into small manageable clusters using florist's tape, before inserting them into the foam blocks.

This creation came into existence thanks to a gorgeous little tyke called Archie. His parents, before he was born, nicknamed him 'little cheese', and asked us to make them a cheesecake for his christening. Little did they know they'd be getting *our* version of a cheesecake — mice and all! We usually buy ready-coloured sugar paste for decorating the cake, but you can tint yours with food colouring paste if needed.

SERVES 20–25

CHEESE & CRACKERS

FOR THE CAKE

- 25 cm (10 inch) round cake
- filling of choice, such as creamy vanilla frosting (page 231) or ganache (page 231); for quantities see page 241
- red sugar paste (rolled fondant), for covering the base board; for quantities see page 239
- yellow sugar paste (rolled fondant), for covering the cake; for quantities see page 239
- brown, black and white sugar paste (rolled fondant), for modelling the mice
- 10 g (¼ oz) CMC gum
- yellow and light brown airbrush colours (optional) or edible dust colours
- sugar glue

YOU WILL ALSO NEED

- 35 cm (14 inch) round base board
- 25 cm (10 inch) round cake board
- airbrush (optional)
- ribbon

First, cover your base board with sugar paste (see page 233). Finish with ribbon trim, then set the board to one side until needed.

Cut each cake horizontally into three equal layers, then place the bottom third on the cake board. Layer the cake with your choice of filling, then dirty-ice (see page 234).

Cut out a generous wedge of cake (to decorate the top of the cake) and set aside.

Before icing the main cake, take a melon baller and cut random pieces out of the cake to create a Swiss-cheese 'hole' effect. Now cover the cake with a layer of yellow sugar paste, about 5 mm (¼ inch) thick (see page 234), smoothing the paste gently into the indents to create the holes. Repeat with the reserved wedge of cake. Place the cake on the covered base board.

Using an airbrush or paintbrush, lightly highlight the holes of the 'cheese' with a darker yellow colour, and then light brown, to create an illusion of depth.

»

»

TO MAKE THE MICE

Mix some brown sugar paste with a little CMC gum. For the body, roll into a long pear shape.

Make two small teardrop-shaped pieces for the feet. Mark the toes with the back of a knife, then flatten slightly to put under the body.

Roll two sausage pieces for the arms. Indent slightly at one side, leaving a small amount at the end to make the hand. Flatten slightly, mark the fingers, then attach the arms to the body.

For the head, roll a ball, shaping one side into a pointy teardrop for the nose. Turn the nose up slightly. Using sugar glue, attach a small ball of black sugar paste at the tip. Cut the mouth opening with a knife. While the paste is still soft, create indents for the eye sockets, using a ball tool. Fill the sockets using a little ball of white sugar paste, placing a little ball of black sugar paste on top. The black ball can be placed anywhere, depending on which direction you'd like the mice to look.

FOR THE CRACKERS

Roll out some sugar paste quite thinly, then cut out 5 cm (2 inch) discs. Create little holes with a toothpick.

Lightly highlight the edges with a light brown colour to make the crackers look golden and just baked. Arrange the mice and crackers around the cake.

CHARACTER CRITTERS

The mice and crackers can be shaped well ahead of time. Make sure you lay them out on pieces of foam to allow them to dry in their correct positions. To give the cake extra character, try to give the mice different expressions and attributes while you are moulding and shaping them.

This cake, displayed in the front window of our shop with antique cutlery protruding from every angle, has created what we call the 'bendy neck'. It lures passers-by to gaze into our window, their necks outstretched as they keep walking by, allowing them a longer look at the cake without actually having to stop. Most of the time the customers are drawn inside, just to take a closer look and find out if it actually *is* a cake.

SERVES 60–70

RUFFLES

FOR THE CAKE

- three 22.5 cm (9 inch) round cakes
- filling of choice, such as creamy vanilla frosting (page 231) or ganache (page 231); for quantities see page 241
- chocolate sugar paste (rolled fondant), for covering the base board and cakes; for quantities see page 239
- sugar glue

YOU WILL ALSO NEED

- 30 cm (12 inch) round base board
- three 22.5 cm (9 inch) round cake boards
- dowels
- cutlery (optional)
- ribbon

First, cover your base board with sugar paste (see page 233). Finish with ribbon trim, then set the board to one side until needed.

Cut each cake horizontally into three equal layers, then place the bottom third of each cake on a cake board of the same size. Layer each cake with your choice of filling, then dirty-ice (see page 234).

You should now have three filled and dirty-iced cake tiers, each with three layers.

Using dowels for support, stack the cake tiers centrally on top of each other (see page 237).

Give the whole cake a final layer of dirty icing. Allow to set for about 10 minutes.

Cover the entire cake with a layer of chocolate sugar paste, about 3 mm (1⁄8 inch) thick (see page 234). Carefully place the cake onto the covered base board, using a palette knife or by placing your hand underneath the cake.

Working with a small quantity at a time, roll out the chocolate sugar paste into strips about 15 cm (6 inches) long and 2 cm (3⁄4 inch) wide. Using the end of your rolling pin, flatten one edge slightly more than the other, to create the ruffles.

Once you have three or four strips ready, paint the thicker edges with sugar glue, then layer them around the cake, gathering them a little to create the ruffles. Repeat the process until the whole cake is covered.

To complete the top of the cake, just twist a few of the strips in every direction, creating an unruly mess. If you wish, you can then finish the cake by inserting assorted cutlery into the top.

QUICK CLUE ON SUGAR GLUE

You can buy sugar glue from cake decorating supply shops, or make your own by mixing some sugar paste or CMC powder with a little hot water.

Lugano
MAJESTIC
HOTEL, WEGGIS
E.M.A.

For the vintage-style wedding that seems to be extremely popular in our neck of the woods, this cake has an elegance that can be personally tailored for each bride. It can be created in beautiful tones of creams, ivory, pale pinks, apricots and mushroomy browns, using lace border moulds in different patterns and sizes, or real lace trimmings to match the bridal dress or theme. This design can be uniquely different every time.

SERVES 80–100

PEARLS & LACE

FOR THE CAKE

- 15 cm (6 inch) round cake
- 22.5 cm (9 inch) round cake
- 30 cm (12 inch) round cake
- filling of choice, such as creamy vanilla frosting (page 231) or ganache (page 231); for quantities see page 241
- sugar paste (rolled fondant), for covering the base board and cakes; for quantities see page 239
- marzipan or almond sugar paste (rolled fondant), for covering the cakes; for quantities see page 239
- 1 quantity of royal icing (page 230)
- sugar glue

YOU WILL ALSO NEED

- 37.5 cm (15 inch) round base board
- 15 cm (6 inch) round cake board
- 22.5 cm (9 inch) round cake board
- 30 cm (12 inch) round cake board
- 17.5 cm (7 inch) foam disc, about 2.5 cm (1 inch) high
- 10 cm (4 inch) foam disc, about 2.5 cm (1 inch) high
- dowels
- a lace mould, or fabric lace and double-sided tape
- shimmer dust
- scriber tool
- pearls
- ribbon

First, cover your base board with sugar paste (see page 233). Finish with ribbon trim, then set the board to one side until needed.

Cut each cake horizontally into three equal layers, then place the bottom third of each cake on a cake board of the same size. Layer each cake with your choice of filling, then dirty-ice (see page 234).

You should now have three filled and dirty-iced cake tiers, each with three layers.

Cover each tier with a layer of marzipan or almond sugar paste, about 3 mm (⅛ inch) thick (see page 234). Leave the cakes out on the bench overnight to set the sugar paste and make it more manageable.

IF USING A LACE MOULD

Cover each tier with another layer of plain sugar paste, about 3 mm (⅛ inch) thick.

Roll out some sugar paste, in the desired colour, into strips the same size as the mould. Place the sugar paste onto the lace mould, pushing it into all the crevices to create the lace effect, then trimming the edges neatly.

»

»

Using sugar glue, paint the sides of the cake and wrap the lace sugar paste design around the cake, making sure to join each piece securely to the next in a consecutive pattern, to prevent a line where they join. Repeat for each tier.

Brush shimmer dust over the pattern to enhance the design.

IF USING FABRIC LACE

Cover each tier with another layer of plain sugar paste, about 5 mm (¼ inch) thick.

Wrap a length of fabric lace around the cake and secure with double-sided tape. Repeat for each tier.

TO FINISH THE CAKE

Take the two bottom tiers and, using a scriber tool, mark out the size of the tier above. Place the pearls around each line, securing them in place with a small dot of royal icing.

Place the largest cake onto the covered base board. Position the 17.5 cm (7 inch) foam block in the centre and hold in place with royal icing.

Place the 10 cm (4 inch) foam block in the centre of the middle cake and secure with royal icing.

Using dowels for support around the foam blocks, and working from largest cake to smallest, stack the cake tiers centrally on top of each other, topping each foam block with more royal icing to secure (see page 237).

Finish with handmade or fresh flowers that are full and fluffy, for that beautiful vintage feel.

The beauty of this design is its simplicity and versatility. You can create any size petals you like, and make the pattern flow how you want it to, over as many tiers as you like. You can also dust the edges of the petals with a different colour to bring the petals to life.

SERVES ABOUT 40

PRETTY PETALS

FOR THE CAKE

- 15 cm (6 inch) round cake
- 17.5 cm (7 inch) round cake
- 20 cm (8 inch) round cake
- filling of choice, such as creamy vanilla frosting (page 231) or ganache (page 231); for quantities see page 241
- sugar paste (rolled fondant), for covering the base board and cakes; for quantities see page 239
- marzipan or almond sugar paste (rolled fondant), for covering the cakes; for quantities see page 239
- 1 quantity of royal icing (page 230)
- 200 g (7 oz) flower paste

YOU WILL ALSO NEED

- 30 cm (12 inch) round base board
- 15 cm (6 inch) round cake board
- 17.5 cm (7 inch) round cake board
- 20 cm (8 inch) round cake board
- piping (icing) bag
- dowels
- pearl string
- 3 cm (1¼ inch), 4 cm (1½ inch) and 5 cm (2 inch) rose-petal cutters
- ball tool (optional)
- ribbon

First, cover your base board with sugar paste (see page 233). Finish with ribbon trim, then set the board to one side until needed.

Cut each cake horizontally into three equal layers, then place the bottom third of each cake on a cake board of the same size. Layer each cake with your choice of filling, then dirty-ice (see page 234).

You should now have three filled and dirty-iced cake tiers, each with three layers.

Cover each tier with a layer of marzipan or almond sugar paste, about 3 mm (⅛ inch) thick (see page 234). Leave the cakes out on the bench overnight to set the sugar paste and make it more manageable.

The next day, cover each cake tier with another layer of plain sugar paste, about 5 mm (¼ inch) thick.

Place the largest cake onto the covered base board. Using dowels for support, and working from largest cake to smallest, stack the cake tiers centrally on top of each other (see page 237).

Finish with ribbon trim and pearl string around the base of each cake tier.

»

»

FOR THE PETALS

Prepare the royal icing and place in a piping (icing) bag.

Roll out the flower paste as thinly as possible. Using the rose-petal cutters, cut out about 60 individual petals.

Taking one petal at a time, use a ball tool (or the back of a spoon or a cocktail stick) to gently smooth over the edges to create an extremely fine edge, leaving the centre the original thickness.

Once you have thinned all the petal edges, attach the petals to the cake tiers by piping a small dot of royal icing on the back of each petal, starting with the bigger petals from the top and bottom edges, working your way towards the centre of the middle tier, creating a nice flow.

Using smaller petals for the centre of the floral arrangement will draw your focus here, so finish with a few pearls if you like. We have used mostly larger petals, with just a few smaller petals for the centre.

SIMPLY EXQUISITE

Flower paste, available from cake decorating stores, is a form of icing that is specially made for creating flower shapes. As it can be rolled very thinly and is easy to work with, it will make decorating this cake seem effortless.

If you like, you can colour the flower paste before covering the cake, making the petals a more dominant feature.

The use of edible gold/silver leaf will also enhance the cake's sophistication.

GUARISCE:
par Xavier Gosé
Lever au Coucher
par René Maizeroy
MON FILM
VACANCES ROMAINES
IL MATTINO ILLUSTRATO
CITROEN
ITALIANA
L'enragé
MON FILM
Avril à Paris
ACROBATE
LA BAIONNETTE
P.A.L.
J. POTIER, LECORSIER & Cie
LA VIE PARISIENNE
RUSTICA
L'Assiette au Beurre
LA DOMENICA DEL CORRIERE
Ciné-Miroir
Le Rire
Le Petit Journal
Le Chanteur des Rues

This is the most talked-about cake in the shop. Standing five tiers tall, its elegance is astounding, its whimsical airiness created by the use of feather-like triangles of rice paper. Most customers cannot believe it is all edible... although rice paper is not the tastiest!

SERVES 100–120

FEATHER CAKE

FOR THE CAKE

- 10 cm (4 inch) round cake
- 15 cm (6 inch) round cake
- 20 cm (8 inch) round cake
- 25 cm (10 inch) round cake
- 30 cm (12 inch) round cake
- filling of choice, such as creamy vanilla frosting (page 231) or ganache (page 231); for quantities see page 241
- sugar paste (rolled fondant), for covering the base board and cakes; for quantities see page 239
- 1 quantity of royal icing (page 230)
- 36 sheets of rice paper, measuring about 15 x 25 cm (6 x 10 inches)
- edible glitter

YOU WILL ALSO NEED

- 35 cm (14 inch) round base board
- 10 cm (4 inch) round cake board
- 15 cm (6 inch) round cake board
- 20 cm (8 inch) round cake board
- 25 cm (10 inch) round cake board
- 30 cm (12 inch) round cake board
- dowels
- piping (icing) bag
- ribbon

First, cover your base board with sugar paste (see page 233). Finish with ribbon trim, then set the board to one side until needed.

Cut each cake horizontally into three equal layers, then place the bottom third of each cake on a cake board of the same size. Layer each cake with your choice of filling, then dirty-ice (see page 234).

You should now have five filled and dirty-iced cake tiers, each with three layers.

Cover each cake tier with a layer of sugar paste, about 5 mm (¼ inch) thick (see page 234).

Place the largest cake onto the covered base board. Using dowels for support, and working from the largest cake to the smallest, stack the cake tiers centrally on top of each other (see page 237).

Prepare the royal icing and place in a piping (icing) bag.

Cut each sheet of rice paper into isosceles triangles, measuring about 2.5 cm (1 inch) at the base, and 12.5 cm (5 inches) along the sides.

Pipe royal icing onto the base of each triangle and spiral the triangles around the cake in layers.

For the very top, overlay each triangle around your finger or rolling pin – you'll need about 20 triangles all up – to get one large round of triangles stuck together by royal icing. Place in the middle of the top tier.

Finish with ribbon trim around the base of the cake. Dust with a little edible glitter to give it that extra sparkle.

CRÈME DE LA CRÈME

These cakes have been our heroes in both New York and London, adorning afternoon tea stands before being whisked table side. If butter cake is the origin of the species, then these are the higher life forms of the cake world.

The creamy layered cake creations in this chapter pay homage to the great French masters. If butter cake is the origin of the species, then these are the higher life forms of the cake world.

These cakes have been our heroes in both New York and London, adorning afternoon tea stands before being whisked table side. The best thing about this style of cake is that it is relatively easy to get diverse flavour and texture combinations.

We garnish most of our cakes on the tray they are served on, with easy crispy bits or a mere smear of mirror glaze, and leave the bits on the tray that fall there. Our excuse is if it works for Donna Hay — the woman who redefined Australian food styling — well it might just work for us!

When making creamy layered cakes, put your thinking cap on and work out which flavours you want to be pronounced, then add some crunchy and chewy bits to make the eating exciting. If you want the cake to be rich and satisfying, make the mousse element heavy and cloying so your guests will never again yearn for that sweet indulgence — or play with whimsical flavour pairings that will make their palates drift to summer tea parties under drooping willows.

All the mousses and jellies in this chapter could be used on their own, so feel free to pipe them into individual serving glasses and forgo the need for cake rings and acetate. Mix and match sponges with mousses, and soak sponges with your favourite liqueur to make a cake that screams uniquely of you.

This is another one of those occasions where a little 'time lapse' will make your life easier. Setting the jelly layers and making the sponge the day before assembling with the mousse will make the process a whole lot simpler, and the sponge and jelly will also be a lot easier to handle.

If you are planning a party that is still a week away, make the whole cake a week in advance and pull it from the freezer the day before you need it. Your guests will never know and will applaud your baking prowess.

This cake reminds me of summer trips to Paris and all its lovely cake shops, where overindulging is an art form and a pleasure. When Michelin-starred chef Angela Hartnett added a cake trolley to the afternoon tea service at the Connaught hotel in London, this was the star of the show. This cake is never, ever going to come off our shop menu. It's an absolute favourite.

MAKES ONE 20 CM (8 INCH) CAKE

FRAMBOISE

RASPBERRY JELLY

10 g (¼ oz) gelatine sheets
300 g (10½ oz) raspberries
55 g (2 oz) caster (superfine) sugar

Spray the outside edge of a 20 cm (8 inch) cake ring with cooking oil. (If you don't have a cake ring, use a loose-based tin without the base.) Tear off a sheet of plastic wrap, about 50 cm (20 inches) long, and fold in half to create a double thickness. Scrunch the plastic wrap around the bottom of the cake ring, pulling it fairly tight to create a 'drum'. Place on a baking tray.

Soak the gelatine in a bowl of cold water for 5 minutes. Drain and squeeze out the excess liquid.

Warm the raspberries and sugar just enough to dissolve the sugar. Add the gelatine and stir to dissolve and ensure there are no lumps.

Pour the jelly into the cake tin and leave to set in the fridge for 1 hour; the jelly can be made several days ahead.

PISTACHIO SPONGE

100 g (3½ oz) pistachio nuts
100 g (3½ oz) icing (confectioners') sugar
2 eggs
6 egg whites
60 g (2¼ oz) caster (superfine) sugar
70 g (2½ oz) plain (all-purpose) flour

Preheat the oven to 175°C (345°F/Gas 3–4). Line a baking tray with baking paper. Lightly grease the inside of a 20 cm (8 inch) cake ring and place on the baking tray.

Place the pistachios in a food processor and blend to a fine powder. Transfer to a mixing bowl, add the icing sugar and whole eggs and whisk to a thick, creamy paste.

In a separate bowl, whisk the egg whites to stiff peaks using a stand mixer. Add the sugar in a few additions and keep whisking until you have a smooth, shiny meringue.

Gently fold the meringue into the pistachio mixture and follow with the flour, being careful not to overwork.

Pour the sponge into the cake ring and bake for 15 minutes, or until firm. Leave to cool.

CRÈME FRAÎCHE MOUSSE

6 g (1⁄6 oz) gelatine sheets
300 ml (10½ fl oz) thin (pouring) cream
2 egg yolks
60 g (2¼ oz) caster (superfine) sugar
150 g (5½ oz) crème fraîche
grated zest of 3 lemons

Soak the gelatine in a bowl of cold water for 5 minutes. Drain and squeeze out the excess liquid.

Using an electric mixer, lightly whip the cream to soft peaks.

Set a heatproof bowl over a saucepan of simmering water, ensuring the base of the bowl doesn't touch the water. Add the egg yolks and sugar to the bowl. Using hand-held electric beaters, whisk until the yolks are warm, pale and creamy.

Remove from the heat, add the drained gelatine and stir to dissolve. Fold in the crème fraîche and lemon zest, followed by the cream.

TO ASSEMBLE

Line a 20 cm (8 inch) cake ring with acetate, so that the finished cake will slide out easily. Place on a baking tray.

Slice the sponge horizontally into two even layers and place one disc in the bottom of the cake ring.

Portion the mousse into three equal amounts. Place one portion onto the first layer of sponge and smooth it out.

Run to the fridge and grab the raspberry jelly. Remove the cake ring and plastic wrap, and place the jelly on top of the mousse.

Top with another portion of mousse, then the other sponge layer. Top with the remaining portion of mousse and level with a palette knife.

Chill for at least 4 hours before serving; the entire cake can be made ahead and frozen for several weeks.

× SMOOTH WORK ×
The sponge and jelly elements can be made a day or two ahead, but the mousse is best prepared just before assembling the cake.

This cake came into being through sheer dumb luck, when we were scrounging about trying to pull a cake together for some friends. Roger McShane and Sue Dyson run an amazing business importing French organic and biodynamic wines, and this cake was for a wine matching. These two are food critics and really know their stuff, so there was nowhere to hide! I think they liked it — but as with all food critics, who *really* knows what the hell they are thinking? I believe they enjoy seeing chefs in constant turmoil.

MAKES ONE 20 CM (8 INCH) CAKE

QUINCY

HAZELNUT DACQUOISE

5 egg whites
a pinch of cream of tartar
50 g (1¾ oz) caster (superfine) sugar
125 g (4½ oz) ground hazelnuts
125 g (4½ oz) icing (confectioners') sugar

Preheat the oven to 200°C (400°F/Gas 6). Whisk the egg whites and cream of tartar in the bowl of a stand mixer until stiff peaks form. Slowly add the caster sugar down the side of the bowl and whisk for 3–4 minutes, or until the meringue is shiny and smooth.

Combine the ground hazelnuts and icing sugar. Using a spatula, gently fold the mixture into the meringue.

Draw two 20 cm (8 inch) circles on two sheets of baking paper. Turn the sheets over and use them to line two baking trays. Deposit half the meringue mixture into the outline of each paper circle, then smooth the top with a palette knife or the back of a spoon. Don't worry too much if the meringue goes over the line, as you can always trim it with a knife prior to assembling the cake.

Bake for 5 minutes, then reduce the oven temperature to 170°C (325°F/Gas 3) and bake for a further 20 minutes, or until the dacquoise feels firm, like a sponge. Remove from the oven and leave to cool on the trays.

Transfer to an airtight container until ready to use; the dacquoise will keep for up to 2 days.

QUINCE JELLY

100 g (3½ oz) caster (superfine) sugar
2 quinces, peeled and cored
10 g (¼ oz) gelatine sheets

Put the sugar and 400 ml (14 fl oz) water in a large saucepan. Add the quinces, then slowly bring to the boil to dissolve the sugar. Cover with a round of baking paper and bring to a slow simmer. Cook, without the lid on, for 6 hours, or until the quinces turn a deep, dark red. Transfer to an airtight container, cover with a round of baking paper, seal the lid and refrigerate until required.

Spray the outside edge of a 20 cm (8 inch) cake ring with cooking oil. (If you don't have a cake ring, use a loose-based tin without the base.) Tear off a sheet of plastic wrap, about 50 cm (20 inches) long, and fold in half to create a double thickness. Scrunch the plastic wrap around the bottom of the cake ring, pulling it fairly tight to create a 'drum'. Place on a baking tray.

Remove the quinces from the poaching liquid, reserving the liquid. Slice the quinces lengthways, about 5 mm (¼ inch) thick, then arrange over the plastic lining of the cake ring.

Soak the gelatine in cold water for 5 minutes. Drain and squeeze out the excess liquid.

Warm 200 ml (7 fl oz) of the reserved quince poaching liquid, add the gelatine and stir to dissolve. Pour the jelly over the fruit and set in the fridge for 1–2 hours to create a nice even layer. The jelly can be made a day or two ahead.

»

»

YOGHURT MOUSSE

3 egg yolks
90 g (3¼ oz) caster (superfine) sugar
9 g (¼ oz) gelatine sheets
finely grated zest of 1 lemon
300 ml (10½ fl oz) thin (pouring) cream
250 g (9 oz) plain yoghurt

Place a heatproof bowl over a saucepan of gently simmering water, ensuring the base of the bowl doesn't touch the water. Gently whisk the egg yolks and sugar in the bowl until pale and creamy.

Meanwhile, soak the gelatine in a bowl of cold water for 5 minutes. Drain and squeeze out the excess liquid, then add to the egg yolks and stir to dissolve. Stir in the lemon zest.

Whip the cream to soft peaks. Gently fold the yoghurt into the egg yolk mixture, followed by the whipped cream.

The mousse is best made just before assembling the cake.

TO ASSEMBLE

50 g (1¾ oz) dark chocolate, melted
3 tablespoons lemon curd (page 221)

Line a 20 cm (8 inch) cake ring with acetate, so that the finished cake will slide out easily. (If you don't have a cake ring, use a loose-based tin without the base.) Ensure your dacquoise fits into the ring; and if not, trim the edges. Place on a baking tray.

Smear the melted chocolate over one of the dacquoise bases. Allow to set briefly, then place the dacquoise in the ring, chocolate side down. (The main purpose of this is to stop the dacquoise sticking to the plate or stand, making the cake more manageable when it comes to eating.)

Dig about in the back of the fridge and pull out some lemon curd. Spread a fine layer over the dacquoise, before placing the second dacquoise on the top and giving it a little press. Add another thin layer of lemon curd, then add half the mousse.

Now take the quince jelly from the fridge and remove the ring and plastic wrap. Place the jelly on top of the cake. Top with the remaining mousse and level with a palette knife.

Chill the cake in the fridge overnight before serving; the entire cake can be made ahead and frozen for several weeks.

To serve, simply remove the cake ring and acetate.

The Golden Gaytime (known as Biscuit Crumble in New Zealand) is the iconic ice cream of our Australian childhood. Essentially it's a toffee and vanilla ice-cream combo, speared onto a wooden stick and covered with a bloody delicious and deliriously addictive honeycomb biscuit coating. This is our dark chocolate tribute to that classic.

MAKES 6

DREAMING OF A CHOCOLATE GAYTIME

CHOCOLATE CRUMBS

90 g (3¼ oz) plain (all-purpose) flour
30 g (1 oz) icing (confectioners') sugar
30 g (1 oz) Dutch-processed cocoa powder
a pinch of bicarbonate of soda (baking soda)
60 g (2¼ oz) cold butter
1 egg

Preheat the oven to 175°C (345°F/Gas 3–4). Put the flour, icing sugar, cocoa, bicarbonate of soda and butter in a bowl. Rub together with your fingertips, until you get a fine crumb, equivalent to Nanna's scones. Add the egg and mix gently to combine.

Roll the mixture between two sheets of baking paper, into 3–4 mm (⅛ inch) crumbs (like a fine gravel). Peel off the top sheet and place the crumbs, still on the bottom sheet, onto a baking tray.

Bake for 15 minutes, then leave to cool.

Crumble the dough into pieces, leaving some bits that are not too fine, as the cake looks better with some extra-large pieces.

Transfer to an airtight container until required; the crumbs can be made up to 1 week ahead.

× SNAPPY SHORTCUT ×
Instead of making the chocolate crumbs, you could simply use some crushed-up chocolate-coated biscuits.

CHOCOLATE PASTRY DISCS

½ quantity of chocolate sweet pastry (page 225)

Preheat the oven to 180°C (350°F/Gas 4). Line a baking tray with baking paper.

Roll the pastry out to about 3 mm (⅛ inch) thick. Using a 6 cm (2½ inch) cutter, cut out six pastry discs. Place on the baking tray and bake for 10 minutes, or until cooked through.

Leave to cool, then transfer to an airtight container until ready to use; the pastry discs will keep for up to 2 days.

CHOCOLATE CRUNCH

20 g (¾ oz) CFC (page 224) or cornflakes
50 g (1¾ oz) chocolate, melted

Mix the CFC or cornflakes and melted chocolate together and give them a bit of a mash with the back of a spoon.

Roll between two sheets of baking paper and leave to set.

Stamp out circles using a 4.5 cm (1¾ inch) cutter and set aside in an airtight container until required; the chocolate crunch circles can be made a day ahead.

»

»

RASPBERRY COMPOTE

150 g (5½ oz) raspberries
2 teaspoons icing (confectioners') sugar

Throw the raspberries in a bowl and smash them up with a back of a fork until you have a lumpy purée. Stir the sugar through, then cover and leave somewhere warm to macerate for a few hours.

CHOCOLATE TRUFFLE MOUSSE

200 g (7 oz) dark chocolate
300 ml (10½ fl oz) thin (pouring) cream

The chocolate truffle mousse should be made just before assembling the cakes.

Roughly chop the chocolate and set aside in a heatproof bowl.

Using an electric mixer, whisk 200 ml (7 fl oz) of the cream until soft peaks form.

Put the remaining cream in a small saucepan, bring to the boil, then pour over the chocolate. Quickly stir until smooth and emulsified, before folding in the whipped cream. Leave for a few minutes to set a little.

TO ASSEMBLE

1 quantity of ganache (page 231)

Line six 5 cm (2 inch) cake rings with acetate, so that the finished cakes will slide out easily.

Place a circle of chocolate crunch in the bottom of each cake ring. Half-fill the cake rings with the mousse. Using a small palette knife, drag the mousse up around the sides to the top edge, to form a chocolate bowl.

Scoop some raspberry compote into the centre of each mould, then top with the remaining mousse. Place the cakes in the freezer for 2 hours to get them ready for coating.

Remove the cakes from the freezer and unmould. Place each one on a little lid or upturned tart mould. Coat in the ganache, then leave for about 5 minutes to set.

One at a time, gently pick up the cakes and coat with the chocolate crumbs. Nestle each cake down on a chocolate pastry disc.

Enjoy straight away, or refrigerate until required. The cakes will keep in the fridge for 2–3 days.

✕ BUDGET BAKEWARE ✕
If you need a whole bunch of cake rings, or the price of the swanky ones leaves you faint with bill shock, do what we did and head to the hardware store, get some water pipe, hack it into lengths with the father-in-law's drop saw, and give them a good clean before using.

MAKES 30 FILLED BISCUITS

OH, PIERRE!

MACARONS

8 egg whites
45 g (1½ oz) caster (superfine) sugar
1 teaspoon egg white powder
325 g (11½ oz) almond meal
500 g (1 lb 2 oz) icing (confectioners') sugar
1 teaspoon raspberry-red food colouring

Line two large baking trays with baking paper.

Using an electric mixer, whisk the egg whites to stiff peaks. Add the sugar gradually, then the egg white powder, whisking to make a nice firm meringue mixture.

Sift the almond meal and icing sugar through a fine sieve. Fold the meringue and the dry ingredients together; keep folding until the mixture falls back into itself without leaving a trace, ensuring all the dry ingredients are well incorporated. You want to keep the mixture on the firmer side, and not too runny; the longer you beat, the runnier it will get. Fold the colouring through.

Put the mixture in a piping (icing) bag fitted with an 8 mm (⅜ inch) plain nozzle. Pipe bulbs about 7 cm (2¾ inches) round onto the lined baking trays, leaving space between each.

Now tap the trays gently – this releases any excess air and flattens the macarons slightly. Allow to sit at room temperature for 30 minutes, or until a skin has formed.

Preheat the oven to 130°C (250°F/Gas 1). Bake the macarons for 10–15 minutes. To check if they are ready, lift one gently from the tray – if it comes clean away from the baking paper, they're good to go.

Allow to cool. The macarons can be frozen in an airtight container between sheets of baking paper for 3–4 weeks.

ROSEWATER JELLY

5 g (⅛ oz) gelatine sheets
20 g (¾ oz) caster (superfine) sugar
25 ml (¾ fl oz) rosewater

Soak the gelatine in a bowl of cold water for 5 minutes, until soft. Meanwhile, warm 100 ml (3½ fl oz) of water in a saucepan.

Squeeze the excess water from the gelatine. Add the gelatine to the warm water, along with the sugar and rosewater. Pour into a small container and set in the fridge for 2 hours.

LAVENDER LYCHEE CREAM

400 ml (14 fl oz) thin (pouring) cream
50 g (1¾ oz) caster (superfine) sugar
3 drops of lavender oil
8 tinned lychees, finely diced

Put all the ingredients in a bowl. Using an electric mixer, whisk to stiff peaks. Place in a piping (icing) bag fitted with a 1 cm (½ inch) nozzle and keep in the fridge until required.

TO ASSEMBLE

300 g (10½ oz) raspberries

Take an upturned macaron and pipe a little lavender lychee cream in the centre. Place a ring of raspberries around the edge, followed by a ring of lavender lychee cream on top the raspberries, leaving a hole in the middle of the lavender lychee cream.

Grab the jelly from the fridge and spoon the rose-scented delight into the centre. Affix another macaron on top and have yourself a moment.

We all have those annoying people in our lives who are much better than us, whom others will always talk about insatiably, as if the pains of living with one's own incompetence and demons weren't enough. Like I dare say a good many other fine pastry chefs, Frenchman Pierre Hermé is the devil. We endure the constant 'oh!'s of customers recounting their recent trip to one of his temple-like establishments, as they describe his latest concoctions, while we hurriedly scribble them down in an attempt to remain relevant. We named this creation after the sighs of his recently returned pilgrims, and now we never tire of hearing punters ask for an 'Oh, Pierre!'

Stan and Julie are two of our favourite customers, and they've hung out wherever Teena has worked in Hobart since we were both apprentices. Back in the day, Julie ordered this cake for Stan's 60th birthday. As it is Stan's favourite cake, we decided to rework it for his 70th birthday. Recently we changed the sponge to be gluten free, adding some variety to our gluten-free selection, which is always challenging.

MAKES ONE 20 CM (8 INCH) CAKE

HAZELNUT CRÈME BRÛLÉE

HAZELNUT SPONGE

100 g (3½ oz) hazelnuts
100 g (3½ oz) icing (confectioners') sugar
2 eggs
9 egg whites
60 g (2¼ oz) caster (superfine) sugar
70 g (2½ oz) gluten-free flour

Preheat the oven to 175°C (345°F/Gas 3–4). Spread the hazelnuts on a baking tray and roast for about 10 minutes, or until deeply coloured. Set aside to cool.

Line a baking tray with baking paper. Lightly grease the inside of a 20 cm (8 inch) cake ring and place on the baking tray.

Place the cooled hazelnuts in a food processor and blend to a fine powder. Transfer to a mixing bowl, add the icing sugar and whole eggs and whisk to a thick, creamy paste.

In a separate bowl, whisk the egg whites to stiff peaks using an electric mixer. Add the sugar in a few additions and keep whisking until you have a smooth, shiny meringue.

Gently fold the meringue into the hazelnut mixture and follow with the flour, being careful not to overwork.

Pour the sponge into the cake ring and bake for 15 minutes, or until firm.

Transfer to an airtight container until ready to use; the sponge can be made a day or two ahead.

CARAMEL BRÛLÉE

7 g (⅙ oz) gelatine sheets
60 g (2¼ oz) caster (superfine) sugar
150 ml (5 fl oz) thin (pouring) cream
150 ml (5 fl oz) milk
3 egg yolks

Spray the outside edge of a 20 cm (8 inch) cake ring with cooking oil. (If you don't have a cake ring, use a loose-based tin without the base.) Tear off a sheet of plastic wrap, about 50 cm (20 inches) long, and fold in half to create a double thickness. Scrunch the plastic wrap around the bottom of the cake ring, pulling it fairly tight to create a 'drum'. Place on a baking tray.

Soak the gelatine in cold water for 5 minutes. Drain and squeeze out the excess liquid. Get a bowl of ice ready for chilling the brûlée.

Meanwhile, place a medium-sized saucepan over high heat and add the sugar. Cook, stirring, for 3–5 minutes, until you have a dark caramel that starts foaming up the pan.

Carefully add the cream a little at a time – beware of splatters, as they can hurt! Lastly, stir in the milk. Return to a simmer, then stir in the egg yolks and cook for about 5 minutes, or until the mixture coats the back of a spoon (83°C/181°F on a sugar thermometer).

Quickly stir in the gelatine, before chilling the mixture over the bowl of ice. Pour the mixture into the lined cake ring, then carefully place in the fridge. Chill for 1 hour to set the brûlée; it can be made a day ahead.

»

»

PRALINE BAVAROIS

12 g (1/3 oz) gelatine sheets
300 ml (10 1/2 fl oz) thin (pouring) cream
200 ml (7 fl oz) milk
50 g (1 3/4 oz) praline paste or hazelnut chocolate spread
40 g (1 1/2 oz) caster (superfine) sugar
5 egg yolks

Soak the gelatine in a bowl of cold water for 5 minutes. Drain and squeeze out the excess liquid. Have a bowl of ice ready for chilling the bavarois.

Using an electric mixer, lightly whip the cream to soft peaks.

Put the milk and praline paste in a saucepan over medium heat and warm to 80°C (176°F) on a sugar thermometer.

In a separate bowl, combine the sugar and egg yolks, then add to the milk mixture and cook for a further 5 minutes, until the mixture coats the back of a spoon (83°C/181°F on a sugar thermometer).

Add the gelatine and stir to dissolve, then chill over the bowl of ice to 50°C (122°F).

Once at 50°C (122°F), add the lightly whipped cream and gently fold through.

TO ASSEMBLE

Line a 20 cm (8 inch) cake ring with acetate, so that the finished cake will slide out easily. Place on a baking tray.

Slice the sponge horizontally into two even layers and place one disc in the bottom of the cake ring.

Portion the praline bavarois into three equal amounts. Place one portion onto the first layer of sponge and smooth it out.

Now upturn the caramel brûlée over the bavarois, then top with another portion of bavarois. Add the other layer of sponge, top with the remaining bavarois and level with a palette knife.

Chill for at least 4 hours before serving.

The entire cake can be made ahead and frozen for several weeks.

THINKING AHEAD
The brûlée and sponge elements can be made a day or two ahead, but the bavarois should be made just before assembling the cake.

Listening to a pastry superstar on the radio, rambling on about how food is like fashion, and that he sees himself as some kind of trendsetting Louis Vuitton fashionista, led to an overwhelming feeling of bewilderment, as though one of the brethren core had turned to the dark side. A flash of lightning, the heralding of trumpets, and we created our 'pear of choux' — the heathen second-cousin to the throne, defiant to the end.

MAKES 12

PEAR OF CHOUX

CRISPY SHORTBREAD SHELL

100 g (3½ oz) butter
100 g (3½ oz) plain (all-purpose) flour
25 g (1 oz) Dutch-processed cocoa powder
125 g (4½ oz) caster (superfine) sugar

In a bowl, rub all the ingredients together to make a smooth paste.

Form into a brick about the width and length of the intended éclairs, so about 12 cm (4½ inches) wide and 3 cm (1¼ inches) high.

Wrap in plastic wrap and chill in the fridge for several hours.

CHOUX PASTRY

100 ml (3½ fl oz) milk
80 g (2¾ oz) butter
10 g (¼ oz) caster (superfine) sugar
½ teaspoon sea salt
120 g (4¼ oz) plain (all-purpose) flour, plus extra for dusting
3 eggs

Put 100 ml (3½ fl oz) of water in a saucepan with the milk, butter, sugar and salt. Bring to the boil.

Add the flour all at once and cook, stirring, over medium heat, for 3–4 minutes, until the bottom of the pan turns white and the mixture comes away from the side of the pan.

Pour the mixture into the bowl of a stand mixer, then mix on low speed until the steam stops rising. Slowly add the eggs, until incorporated.

Lightly grease a baking tray that will fit in your freezer. Dust lightly with flour.

Place the pastry in a piping (icing) bag fitted with a 12 mm (½ inch) nozzle. Pipe into 12 éclairs about 12 cm (4½ inches) long.

Now cut 12 thin slices of the shortbread pastry and place one on top of each éclair.

Freeze for several hours until frozen, or for up to 1 week.

PASSIONFRUIT CUBEB PEARS

5 williams pears
100 ml (3½ fl oz) passionfruit juice
50 g (1¾ oz) caster (superfine) sugar
2 teaspoons freshly ground cubeb pepper or black pepper

Peel the pears and remove the cores using an apple corer.

Put the remaining ingredients in a saucepan with 400 ml (14 fl oz) of water and bring to a simmer. Add the pears and cover with a round of baking paper. Return to a simmer and cook for 20 minutes, or until tender.

Leave to cool in the poaching liquid. The pears can be refrigerated in an airtight container for up to 2 days.

»

"DO NOT EAT"
DESICCANT
SILICA
GEL
THROW AWAY
"DO NOT EAT"
DESICCANT

»

PAIN DE GÊNES (GENOA BREAD)

160 g (5½ oz) marzipan
3 eggs, lightly beaten
50 g (1¾ oz) butter, melted
30 g (1 oz) plain (all-purpose) flour
½ teaspoon baking powder

Preheat the oven to 170°C (325°F/Gas 3). Warm the marzipan in the microwave for 30 seconds, then place in the bowl of a stand mixer fitted with a beater attachment.

Mixing on low speed, slowly add the eggs until you get a smooth batter. Fold in the melted butter, then the flour and baking powder.

Spread the batter out onto a 24 cm (9½ inch) square baking tray lined with baking paper. (If you don't have a baking tray this size, fold the baking paper on the tray to make a receptacle the right size.)

Slice the poached pears as thinly as possible, then arrange on top of the batter, making a pretty pattern if you wish.

Bake for 20 minutes, or until the cake is cooked when tested with a skewer.

CHOCOLATE FOOL

300 ml (10½ fl oz) thin (pouring) cream
50 g (1¾ oz) chocolate sauce or ganache (page 231)

Lightly whip the cream, then tint with the chocolate sauce or ganache. You probably won't need to sweeten the mixture, but go with what you like.

TO ASSEMBLE

Preheat the oven to 180°C (350°F/Gas 4). Place the frozen éclairs on a greased and floured baking tray and bake from frozen for 25 minutes.

Switch the oven off, then place a wooden spoon in the oven door to hold it open a crack. Leave the éclairs to cool in the oven for 20 minutes or so.

Cut a hole in the bottom of the éclairs, then pipe the chocolate fool mixture into the éclairs.

Cut the pain de gênes into portions the same size as your finished éclairs. Use these as your base and sit the éclairs on top.

We like to decorate the éclairs with some little rectangles of milk chocolate.

These éclairs are best enjoyed the same day.

MAKES ONE 20 CM (8 INCH) CAKE

CHUNKY MONKEY

BROWNIE

2 eggs
260 g (9¼ oz) dark brown sugar
90 g (3¼ oz) unsalted butter, melted
50 g (1¾ oz) Dutch-processed cocoa powder
110 g (3¾ oz) plain (all-purpose) flour
1 teaspoon sea salt
60 g (2¼ oz) roasted peanuts

Preheat the oven to 180°C (350°F/Gas 4). Line a baking tray with baking paper. Lightly grease the inside of a 20 cm (8 inch) cake ring and place on the baking tray.

Using an electric mixer, whisk the eggs and sugar until light and fluffy, then slowly add the melted butter.

Sieve the cocoa powder and flour into a separate bowl, then add to the egg mixture all at once with the salt and nuts. Gently fold in.

Pour into the cake ring and bake for 30 minutes, or until just set in the centre. Remove from the oven and leave to cool.

CARAMELISED BANANA JAM

60 g (2¼ oz) caster (superfine) sugar
2 bananas, sliced in half lengthways
1 teaspoon finely grated fresh ginger

Place the sugar in a heavy-based frying pan and stir over high heat until the sugar begins to caramelise.

When it becomes dark and smoky, add the banana and mix well. Add the grated ginger and remove from the heat.

MILK CHOCOLATE MOUSSE

200 g (7 oz) milk chocolate
300 ml (10½ fl oz) thin (pouring) cream
6 g (⅙ oz) gelatine sheets
2 egg yolks
55 g (2 oz) caster (superfine) sugar

Put the chocolate in a heatproof bowl set over a saucepan of simmering water, ensuring the base of the bowl doesn't touch the water. Allow the chocolate to melt, stirring occasionally.

Lightly whip the cream and set aside.

Meanwhile, soak the gelatine in a bowl of cold water for 5 minutes. Drain and squeeze out the excess liquid.

Set a separate heatproof bowl over a saucepan of simmering water. Add the egg yolks and sugar to the bowl. Using hand-held electric beaters, whisk until the yolks are warm, pale and creamy.

Remove from the heat, add the gelatine and stir to dissolve. Add the melted chocolate, then the whipped cream.

TO ASSEMBLE

Cut the brownie out of the ring. Wash the ring, then line with acetate and place on a baking tray. Reinsert the brownie. Using a palette knife, smear the banana jam over the brownie, then top with the mousse.

Chill in the fridge for 3 hours or overnight. The entire cake can be made ahead and frozen for several weeks.

Why 'chunky monkey'? Well, it's simple really... monkeys are brown, monkeys like bananas, and the whole idea is, well, nuts! Definitely make the brownie a day ahead. It's deliciously dense, so cover and store at cool room temperature rather than in the fridge. The caramelised banana jam and mousse are best made just before using.

Vanilla slice is a classic Australian custardy bakery treat, but all too often it's a yellow rubbery mess, with soggy puff pastry and custard so cloying that it is more reminiscent of tyre rubber than a source of afternoon delight. We use a versatile *crémeux* for our vanilla slice, and it is completely freezeable. Making your own butter puff or buying good butter puff pastry will make your vanilla slice all the finer. The big tip is to bake the hell out of the pastry. It needs to be a uniform deep dark brown all the way through. The darker the pastry, the more the butter caramelises, and the better it all tastes.

MAKES 8

ODE TO VANILLA SLICE

VANILLA CRÉMEUX

300 ml (10½ fl oz) milk
300 ml (10½ fl oz) thin (pouring) cream
1 vanilla bean, cut in half lengthways, seeds scraped
8 egg yolks
150 g (5½ oz) caster (superfine) sugar
15 g (½ oz) gelatine sheets

Put the milk, cream and vanilla seeds in a saucepan and bring to the boil. Set aside for 10 minutes to infuse.

Gently mix together the egg yolks and sugar.

Return the pan to the heat and add the egg yolk mixture. Cook over gentle heat for 5 minutes, or until the mixture coats the back of a spoon (83°C/181°F on a sugar thermometer).

Pass the custard through a fine sieve. While the custard is still warm, soak the gelatine in a bowl of cold water for 5 minutes, until soft, then gently squeeze out the excess water before adding to the custard. Stir to dissolve.

Set up a 10 x 30 cm (4 x 12 inch) tray, or use some foil to make a watertight tray of the same size. Pour in the custard, then cover and freeze for 2 hours, until just set.

The custard can be frozen for up to 1 week, and is easier to handle when frozen.

CARAMELISED PUFF PASTRY

500 g (1 lb 2 oz) puff pastry (page 227)
75 g (2½ oz) caster (superfine) sugar

Preheat the oven to 180°C (350°F/Gas 4). Line a baking tray with baking paper.

Evenly roll out the pastry into a 25 x 35 cm (10 x 14 inch) rectangle, then place on the baking tray. Using a fork or docking wheel, prick the pastry all over – this will make the pastry rise evenly (and we're not looking for masses of lift). Gently moisten with a little water, either with a pastry brush or atomiser bottle, and scatter with half the sugar.

Bake for 20 minutes, then remove from the oven.

At this point it gets a little tricky. Place another sheet of baking paper on the puff pastry. Place a second tray on top, then turn the whole thing over so up is down, and down is up.

Return to the oven and bake for another 30 minutes.

Remove the top tray and baking paper. Scatter the remaining sugar over the pastry and continue to bake for a further 5 minutes, or until the sugar has caramelised.

Remove from the oven and leave to cool, ready to be custified.

The pastry is best cooked just before assembling the slice.

LAVENDER CREAM

400 ml (14 fl oz) thin (pouring) cream
50 g (1¾ oz) caster (superfine) sugar
3 drops of lavender oil

Using an electric mixer, whisk the cream, sugar and lavender oil to stiff peaks.

Place in a piping (icing) bag fitted with a 1 cm (½ inch) nozzle.

TO ASSEMBLE

We normally make individual portions, as the custard tends to self-capitulate if you make one giant slice! This is how we do ours.

Remove the custard from the freezer and slice it into eight portions. Using a serrated knife, trim the edges of the puff pastry, then cut the pastry into two strips that are each about 10 cm (4 inches) wide and 30 cm (12 inches) long.

Place a portion of the custard on the pastry, then cut away that portion of pastry. Repeat to give eight pieces of puff pastry with custard sitting on top.

Pipe a 'skirt' of lavender cream all the way around the edge of each custard.

At this point we add some runny jam or some other little surprise, before topping with some more puff pastry.

We normally finish the top with soft fondant icing, but that can be tricky! Water icing (see the Mrs Ruby recipe on page 115) or just icing (confectioners') sugar is what we use on this number when at home.

The slice will keep for up to 2 days, but is best enjoyed on the day of making.

This is a classic — the 'old school' way of making opera cake. There are modern fancy versions with extra-light, swanky, ethereal mousses, but this is not one of them. We used to make this at the Sofitel hotel in Melbourne, and it was like a marine hazing ritual every time we had to make those fourteen-layer monoliths. Trust me: pull this one off and the heavens will open up, the angels will sing, and your friends will be so dumbfounded by your cooking prowess, they'll probably offer up life-long servitude in exchange for a mere morsel. See, now it seems worth it!

MAKES ONE 20 CM (8 INCH) CAKE

OPERA

JACONDE SPONGE

5 eggs
175 g (6 oz) almond meal
175 g (6 oz) icing (confectioners') sugar
5 egg whites
25 g (1 oz) caster (superfine) sugar
50 g (1¾ oz) plain (all-purpose) flour
40 g (1½ oz) butter, melted

Preheat the oven to 200°C (400°F/Gas 6). Line several baking trays with baking paper.

In a large bowl, whisk together the eggs, almond meal and icing sugar.

In a separate bowl, whisk the egg whites to stiff peaks using an electric mixer. Now add the caster sugar in a few additions, whisking continuously until you have a smooth, shiny meringue.

Fold the meringue into the almond mixture, followed by the flour, and lastly the melted butter.

Divide the batter into five portions. Using a palette knife, spread each portion out into a very thin, even layer onto one of the baking trays, into a 20 cm (8 inch) square, about 3 mm (⅛ inch) thick.

Transfer to the oven and bake for 4 minutes. (Depending on how many baking trays you have, you may need to cook the batter in a few batches until you have five beautiful thin layers of sponge. Your batter will be fine to sit if you need to bake the sponges in batches, as the baking time is very quick.)

Once baked, carefully but immediately remove each sponge from the trays to ensure they don't end up a cornflake, as the residual heat from the tray will keep cooking this super-thin sponge.

The sponges can be made a day ahead. Store them, separated by sheets of baking paper so they don't stick together, with another sheet of baking paper on top, all wrapped in plastic wrap.

GANACHE

450 g (1 lb) dark couverture chocolate, chopped
450 ml (16 fl oz) thin (pouring) cream
30 g (1 oz) liquid glucose
50 g (1¾ oz) butter, at room temperature

Put the chocolate in a heatproof bowl. Bring the cream and glucose to the boil in a small saucepan, then pour over the chocolate and leave to rest for 2 minutes.

Use a hand whisk to lightly remove any lumps and emulsify the mixture into a smooth, shiny ganache, without aerating it too much, as you don't want air bubbles. Add the butter and stir until shiny and smooth.

Leave the ganache at room temperature, ready for assembling. It can sit for a few hours; you can stir it together or warm it gently to make it glossy and smooth just before using.

»

»

COFFEE BUTTER CREAM

120 g (4¼ oz) caster (superfine) sugar
4 egg whites
450 g (1 lb) butter, at room temperature
100 ml (3½ fl oz) good-quality strong coffee (ristretto shots, if possible)

Put the sugar and 60 ml (2 fl oz/¼ cup) of water in a saucepan. Bring to the boil and cook to the soft-ball stage (118°C/245°F on a sugar thermometer).

Using a stand mixer, whisk the egg whites until stiff peaks form, then carefully add the sugar syrup down the side of the bowl. Whisk for a further 10 minutes, until the mixture is glossy and has cooled down to 50°C (122°F) on a sugar thermometer.

Gradually add the butter and mix on low speed until smooth and homogenous. Add the coffee for a punch of coffee deliciousness.

The butter cream can sit for a few hours; beat it a little to soften it just before using.

COFFEE SOAK

50 g (1¾ oz) sugar
200 ml (7 fl oz) hot, strong good-quality coffee

Add the sugar to the coffee while it is still warm and stir to dissolve.

TO ASSEMBLE

50 g (1¾ oz) dark chocolate, melted

Smear the melted chocolate on one of the sponge sheets. We build this cake freeform, so put the sponge, chocolate side down, on a tray, and let's begin the build.

Divide the coffee butter cream into four portions, and the ganache into five portions.

Using the coffee soak and a pastry brush, soak the sponge layer that is sitting on the tray. Spread it with a layer of butter cream.

Follow this with a layer of ganache, making sure the ganache doesn't tear the butter cream – you may need to warm the ganache a little in between.

Now it's simply a case of repeating the steps.

Lastly, top with ganache only, as the final layer.

Leave to set for an hour or so before trimming the edges to reveal your handiwork.

Eating the trimmings is somewhat of a rite of passage, so slow down, grab a cuppa and enjoy your success.

PERFECT ENSEMBLE
The cake will keep in the fridge for up to 3 days; remove from the fridge a few hours before serving to bring it back to room temperature. The cake can also be frozen for a few weeks – just leave off the top ganache layer and add it on the day of serving.

Dining at one of Dan Hong's Sydney restaurants, Ms. G's, we tasted his iconic pandan, strawberry and coconut pudding. On our return home, this concoction was the result. For weeks the cake remained unnamed as we tossed around different ideas, until one sleepless night, watching some really bad kung-fu movies on late-night television, inspiration hit and this name stuck.

MAKES ONE 20 CM (8 INCH) CAKE

CROUCHING STRAWBERRY, HIDDEN PANDAN

ALMOND SPONGE

55 g (2 oz) icing (confectioners') sugar
55 g (2 oz) almond meal
1 egg
3 egg whites
30 g (1 oz) caster (superfine) sugar
45 g (1½ oz) plain (all-purpose) flour

Preheat the oven to 175°C (345°F/Gas 3–4). Draw a 20 cm (8 inch) circle on a sheet of baking paper. Turn the paper over and use to line a baking tray.

Put the icing sugar, almond meal and whole egg in a mixing bowl and whisk together until pale and creamy.

Using a stand mixer, whisk the egg whites until stiff peaks form, then slowly add the caster sugar until you have a smooth, shiny meringue.

Fold the meringue into the almond mixture, then gently fold in the flour.

Spoon the sponge onto the baking paper circle and smooth the top. Bake for 10 minutes, then transfer to a cooling rack.

Store in an airtight container until ready to use; the sponge will keep for up to 2 days.

COCONUT PANDAN DACQUOISE

50 g (1¾ oz) almond meal
50 g (1¾ oz) dessicated (shredded) coconut
60 g (2¼ oz) icing (confectioners') sugar
3 egg whites
a pinch of cream of tartar
25 g (1 oz) caster (superfine) sugar
2 teaspoons pandan paste

Preheat the oven to 200°C (400°F/Gas 6). Draw a 20 cm (8 inch) circle on a sheet of baking paper. Turn the paper over and use to line a baking tray.

Combine the almond meal, coconut and icing sugar and set aside.

Whisk the egg whites and cream of tartar in the bowl of a stand mixer until stiff peaks form. Slowly add the caster sugar down the side of the bowl and whisk for 3–4 minutes, or until the meringue is shiny and smooth.

Add the pandan paste and watch the meringue turn vibrant green. Using a spatula, gently fold the coconut mixture into the meringue.

Deposit the meringue mixture onto the baking paper circle, then smooth the top with a palette knife or the back of a spoon. Don't worry too much if the meringue goes over the line, as you can always trim with a knife prior to assembling the cake.

»

»

Bake for 5 minutes, then reduce the oven temperature to 170°C (325°F/Gas 3) and bake for a further 20 minutes, or until the dacquoise feels firm, like a sponge. Remove from the oven and leave to cool on the tray.

Transfer to an airtight container until ready to use; the dacquoise will keep for up to 2 days.

PASSIONFRUIT AND STRAWBERRY MOUSSE

8 g (1⁄6 oz) gelatine sheets
200 ml (7 fl oz) thin (pouring) cream
2 egg yolks
60 g (2¼ oz) sugar
100 g (3½ oz) passionfruit purée
100 g (3½ oz) strawberry purée

Soak the gelatine in cold water for 5 minutes. Drain and squeeze out the excess liquid.

In a separate bowl, whip the cream until soft peaks form.

Set a heatproof bowl over a saucepan of simmering water, ensuring the base of the bowl doesn't touch the water. Add the egg yolks and sugar to the bowl and whisk until pale and creamy, using hand-held electric beaters.

Add the passionfruit purée and continue cooking for about 5 minutes, until the mixture coats the back of a spoon (83°C/181°F on a sugar thermometer).

Add the gelatine to the passionfruit sabayon, then fold the strawberry purée through, followed by the whipped cream.

COCONUT JELLY

5 g (⅛ oz) gelatine sheets
100 ml (3½ fl oz) coconut cream
10 g (¼ oz) caster (superfine) sugar

Soak the gelatine in cold water for 5 minutes. Drain and squeeze out the excess liquid.

Warm the coconut cream with the sugar. Add the gelatine and stir until dissolved. Allow to cool to room temperature.

TO ASSEMBLE

50 g (1¾ oz) dark chocolate, melted
50 g (1¾ oz) strawberry jam

Line a 20 cm (8 inch) cake ring with some acetate, so that the finished cake will slide out easily. (If you don't have a cake ring, use a loose-based tin without the base.) Ensure your dacquoise fits into the ring; if it doesn't, trim the dacquoise edges. Place on a baking tray.

Smear the melted chocolate over the base of the dacquoise. Allow to set briefly, then place the dacquoise in the ring, chocolate side down. (The main purpose of this is to stop the dacquoise sticking to the plate or stand, making the cake more manageable when it comes to eating.)

Smear the dacquoise with the strawberry jam, then place the almond sponge on top. Add the mousse and set the cake in the fridge for at least 4 hours, or overnight.

Float the coconut jelly on top of the cake. Chill for a further 1 hour before unmoulding.

The cake will keep in an airtight container in the fridge for 1–2 days.

B

I SCREAM

When we first opened, we were sent a link to Humphry Slocombe, the San Francisco godfathers of ice-cream salvation. Ahh, sweet revelation: the heavens opened and our minds exploded. Anything is possible, so let's experiment...

Teena and I have an obsession with ice cream. As soon as we returned from New York, we bought an old water-cooled Carpigiani ice-cream machine that had been advertised in the *Trading Post*. The owner lived way out in country Victoria, but Teena plied a friend of the family to have it picked up.

When we first plugged the machine in, it tripped the fuse. Oh no, we've bought a dud! My youngest brother Elliott, then a second-year apprentice electrician, pulled it apart and declared the European contraption worthy of the trash heap only. We ploughed on, and finally found a three-phase outlet that wouldn't pop, so we were on the way.

I was raised in a devoutly religious household. Dinner would be served as if by clockwork at 6.30 and was not complete until your plate was empty. Dinner time was very austere as my parents, two grandparents, two dogs, three cats and six children gathered around the table. Oh, but on Fridays — the highlight of the week — my nan Kath would arrive in her hot-pink Volkswagen to take us to the milk bar and let us run wild. We never had shop-bought products as kids, so this was a time to wolf down a Buffalo Bill or double-choc wedge: pure indulgence.

Nan's face would light up as we ate the ice cream, and she giggled excitedly at the oncoming sugar rush. It was the beginning of a beautiful obsession.

Ice cream was originally a way for us to use the left-over egg yolks from all the macarons we ended up making — but nowadays the demand for ice cream leaves us with a lot of egg whites! When we first opened, Pat Nourse of *Gourmet Traveller* magazine swung by and liked our ice cream enough to send us a link to Humphry Slocombe, the San Francisco godfathers of ice-cream salvation. Ahh, sweet revelation: the heavens opened and our minds exploded. Anything is possible, so let's experiment... we even let the shockers through to the customers so they can enjoy the laugh of trying to sell a horrifying concoction.

At home we like to add a little gelatine to help capture some air, and we use a fair bit of dextrose monohydrate. Before you gasp that this sounds a little too molecular, head to the beer-brewing aisle of the supermarket and there you will find some. It will give your ice-cream concoctions a smooth creaminess.

Otherwise, there are no rules: just create a flavour and eat it!

This is far and away the most popular ice cream in the shop. Creamy, salty and nutty, its success is really no surprise. Without the additions, the ice cream makes a great vanilla base, through which you could fold any of your favourite toppings, cake scraps or crispy bits.

SERVES 4–6

SALTY ALMOND CARAMEL

200 ml (7 fl oz) thin (pouring) cream
300 ml (10½ fl oz) milk
1 vanilla bean, cut in half lengthways, seeds scraped
6 egg yolks
120 g (4¼ oz) caster (superfine) sugar
½ quantity of salty caramel (page 220)
1 quantity of caramelised nuts (page 224), made using almonds

Put the cream, milk and vanilla bean and seeds in a saucepan. Heat gently until the mixture comes to a simmer, then remove from the heat and leave to infuse for 30 minutes.

Return the pan to medium-high heat. Mix the egg yolks and sugar together in a bowl, but do not over-aerate. Add the egg yolk mixture to the pan and stir until the mixture coats the back of a spoon (83°C/181°F on a sugar thermometer).

Pass the mixture through a fine sieve, into a bowl set over ice.

Once the mixture has chilled, churn in your ice-cream machine as per the manufacturer's instructions.

As soon as the ice cream is ready in the machine, fold the salty caramel and almonds through, making sure to leave some chunks, so that when it comes to the eating, it'll be like finding pots of gold in your ice cream.

The ice cream will keep in the freezer for up to 4 weeks.

This ice cream is the result of some customers being gluttons for punishment. It dishes up a curious dichotomy of heat and cold, with the ice cream feeling cold only while you are licking it. Once the ice cream runs out, you will probably need another scoop of something a little more soothing! This may well be our greatest moment, or our biggest blunder... depending on whether or not you would get the seconds.

MAKES 500 ML (17 FL OZ/2 CUPS)

THE WIDOW MAKER

1 dried cascabel chilli
1 dried ancho chilli
1 dried jalapeño chilli
1 dried chipotle chilli
200 ml (7 fl oz) coconut cream
grated zest and juice of 2 limes
3 g (1⁄10 oz) gelatine sheets
75 g (2½ oz) caster (superfine) sugar
35 g (1¼ oz) dextrose monohydrate

SHAKE SHAKE SHAKE
If you're without an ice-cream machine, or lacking the funds to buy one, grab yourself some zip-lock bags. Pour some ice-cream mixture into one of them and seal it up tightly. Place it in the second bag, along with plenty of ice and about 70 g (2½ oz/½ cup) of salt. Just to be on the safe side, seal it all up in a third zip-lock bag. Now shake the whole thing (get the kids involved!) and in 10 minutes you'll have ice cream.

Remove any stems from the chillies. Warm the chillies in a saucepan with the coconut cream and 170 ml (5½ fl oz/⅔ cup) of water. Simmer for about 10 minutes, or until the chillies are tender. Using a stick bender, whiz the chillies into the coconut cream until you have a smooth liquid that is pretty much lump free. Stir in the lime zest and juice.

Soak the gelatine in cold water for 5 minutes, or until soft and pliable. Remove the gelatine from the water. Squeeze out any excess water, then add the gelatine to the saucepan and stir to dissolve.

Combine the sugar and dextrose, then stir through the coconut cream mixture. Remove from the heat, then strain into a bowl and cool over ice.

Cover and leave to infuse in the fridge overnight to get the most from this evil concoction. Then churn the mixture in an ice-cream machine, as per the manufacturer's instructions.

The ice cream will keep in the freezer for up to 4 weeks.

The naturopath in North Hobart (or 'NoHo', as locals call the suburb) sent a request for coffee ice cream, due to a serious lack of caffeine-induced licking. Banter ensued, with all sorts of wild claims as to the medicinal purposes of *real* coffee ice cream, which kept us in rapturous laughter at the idea of pawning ice-creamy pharmaceuticals. We make this ice cream with a nod to the Vietnamese, who sip their coffee with condensed milk, and add chicory for a 1970s hippy feel to the whole malarkey. You will never lick the same again.

MAKES 1 LITRE (35 FL OZ/4 CUPS)

EL GORDO LOS VIETNAMITAS

300 ml (10½ fl oz) milk
200 ml (7 fl oz) thin (pouring) cream
50 g (1¾ oz) full-bodied roasted coffee beans (we love El Gordo, roasted by the superstars at Melbourne's Seven Seeds)
a pinch of ground chicory tea
50 ml (1½ fl oz) condensed milk
100 g (3½ oz) sugar
6 egg yolks

Warm the milk and cream in a saucepan, along with the coffee beans and chicory. Set aside to infuse for about 30 minutes. Then, using a stick blender, break up most of the coffee beans, blending until the milk is tinged brown with coffee colour.

Mix together the condensed milk, sugar and egg yolks, but do not over-aerate. Set aside.

Stir the egg-yolk mixture into the infused milk and cream. Cook slowly until the mixture coats the back of a spoon (83°C/181°F on a sugar thermometer).

Remove the pan from the heat and pour the mixture through a fine sieve, into a bowl. Place the bowl over ice to chill.

Once cool, you can churn the mixture immediately, but the flavours will be better if left another day in the fridge before churning.

Churn the mixture in an ice-cream machine, as per the manufacturer's instructions.

The ice cream will keep in the freezer for up to 4 weeks.

FAT ELVIS

As a random tip, on Elvis nights, this ice cream is awesome with some smoked lard added towards the end of churning. Red-eye-gravy-inspired and slapped with banana in a split or the like, it's our version of a Fat Elvis!

GRANULATED

Chris Wisbey and Sally Dakis have an amazing farm in Richmond, about 20 minutes from Hobart. Chris has always been especially generous to the shop, and has traded some of his amazing strawberries with us ever since we started. Chris's mum cleans the second-grade berries and freezes them in 1 kilogram bags, which is terribly kind and convenient. Their strawberries are some of the tastiest we've ever had, and the numbing effect of sichuan pepper only seems to enhance their flavour.

MAKES ABOUT 1 LITRE (35 FL OZ/4 CUPS)

STRAWBERRY SICHUAN

10 sichuan peppercorns
5 g (1⁄8 oz) gelatine sheets
60 g (2¼ oz) dextrose monohydrate
110 g (3¾ oz) caster (superfine) sugar
400 g (14 oz) fresh strawberries

Grind the peppercorns using a mortar and pestle. Place in a saucepan with 190 ml (6½ fl oz) of water and allow to warm through.

Soak the gelatine in cold water for 5 minutes, or until soft and pliable. Remove from the water, squeeze out the excess liquid and add the gelatine to the pan.

Mix the dextrose and sugar together, then add to the pan. Add the strawberries and bring to a simmer. There is no need to cook them for long; about 5 minutes will do. Now grab a stick blender and blend the mixture into a smooth purée.

Chill in a bowl set over ice, before churning in your ice-cream machine, as per the manufacturer's instructions.

The sorbet will keep in the freezer for up to 4 weeks.

PASS THE PEPPER

Other interesting peppers that work really well with fruit are cubeb and espalette – well worth trying to add a little zing. Look for them in good spice shops.

This is where it all began. Funnily enough, the first time I made this ice confection in London it was unanimously rejected, never to appear again. Hey, well, it's our shop and I like it, and our customers revel in its honeycomb flavour too. The iconic Tasmanian leatherwood honey is too overpowering for this ice cream, so we use local prickly box honey, which is produced from native bees and has a slight butterscotch flavour. If you can't get your hands on prickly box, try a mild, light honey to get the most from this recipe.

MAKES ABOUT 1 LITRE (35 FL OZ/4 CUPS)

BURNT HONEY ICE CREAM

180 g (6 oz) honey
300 ml (10½ fl oz) thin (pouring) cream
300 ml (10½ fl oz) milk
8 egg yolks

Put the honey in a medium-sized saucepan and begin to warm it over medium heat. At this point it is advisable to turn on your extractor fan, as the honey gets a little smoky.

Cook the honey until it really begins to smoke and is a deep, dark caramel colour; this will take 5–10 minutes.

Slowly add the cream in a few additions and stir with a good long spoon, as hot splatters on the skin can put a slight downer on the day.

Follow the cream with the milk, and warm the mixture to 80°C (176°F) on a sugar thermometer.

Remove the pan from the heat. Lightly whisk the egg yolks, then stir them into the cream mixture. Return to the heat and continue to cook until the mixture coats the back of a spoon (83°C/181°F on a sugar thermometer).

Pass the ice cream through a fine sieve, into a bowl set over ice. Stir occasionally until chilled.

Churn in your ice-cream machine, as per the manufacturer's instructions.

The ice cream will keep in the freezer for up to 4 weeks.

PAN
TADEUSZ
Wódka
ZIELONA GÓRA
1999. 500ml
SMIRNOFF.
Nº 21
Triple Distilled
VODKA

Okay, the Moscow mule is one of the great summertime drinks to soothe the beast from the beating sun ... and 'Donkey!' is the catch-cry in Gordon Ramsay kitchens for anyone who trips in front of the blond-haired assassin. This sorbet is a tribute to all who have fallen, and to those hot summer nights. You could well remove the nip of vodka — but since when does a little nip count... or even the first nip count?

MAKES ENOUGH FOR 8 ADULTS TO ADD TO COCKTAILS ON A SUMMER'S DAY, OR TO SOOTHE ONE SUNBURNT FOOL

VIRGIN RUSSIAN DONKEY

200 ml (7 fl oz) lime juice
160 g (5½ oz) caster (superfine) sugar
35 g (1¼ oz) dextrose monohydrate
5 g (⅛ oz) gelatine sheets
2 cm (¾ inch) chunk of fresh ginger, peeled and finely grated
30 ml (1 fl oz) vodka

Warm the lime juice with 260 ml (9¼ fl oz) of water. Combine the sugar and dextrose and whisk into the lime mixture.

Soak the gelatine in cold water for 5 minutes, or until soft and pliable. Remove from the water, squeeze out the excess liquid and add the gelatine to the warm liquid. Stir in the ginger, followed by the vodka.

Cool in a bowl over ice, before churning in your ice-cream machine, as per the manufacturer's instructions.

The sorbet will keep in the freezer for up to 4 weeks.

We love the flavour of cherry cola — our iconic American arsenic-loving friend. Our pals Chris and Sally have some morello cherry trees at the end of their orchard. Every year, by their good grace, we get some of those sweet cherries and make this sorbet. To extract the juice from the whole fruit, we throw the cherries into a vegetable juicer/centrifuge. The best part is that we get some of the cherry pits in the mix, which crack and release the almondy arsenic flavour that makes this pink concoction a truly Tuff Man dish.

MAKES 1 LITRE (35 FL OZ/4 CUPS)

CHERRY SODA POP

200 ml (7 fl oz) cola
470 ml (16½ fl oz) morello cherry juice
½ cinnamon stick
5 g (⅛ oz) gelatine sheets
80 g (2¾ oz) caster (superfine) sugar
50 g (1¾ oz) dextrose monohydrate

Bring the cola to the boil in a saucepan, then cook until reduced to 50 ml (1½ fl oz).

Add the cherry juice and cinnamon and bring to a simmer. Remove from the heat and set aside to infuse for about 30 minutes.

Soak the gelatine in cold water for 5 minutes, or until soft and pliable. Remove the gelatine from the water and squeeze out any excess liquid. Add the gelatine to the pan and stir until dissolved.

Combine the sugar and dextrose and stir through the mixture. Cool in a bowl set over ice. Discard the cinnamon stick.

Churn the mixture in your ice-cream machine, as per the manufacturer's instructions.

The sorbet will keep in the freezer for up to 4 weeks.

We made this ice cream for a masterclass at The Agrarian Kitchen, a small seasonal cooking school set on a farm in the Derwent Valley, about 45 minutes from Hobart. It is still, to date, our greatest day of ice-cream triumph. The guests milked Pretty Girl, the farm goat, of her creamy goodness, ready to create the ice cream that made our summer. It was the crowning glory of a 2.4-metre-long sundae that we gorged upon as recompense for our strenuous day in the kitchen.

MAKES ABOUT 1 LITRE (35 FL OZ/4 CUPS)

GOAT'S MILK, TAHINI & HONEY ICE CREAM

300 ml (10½ fl oz) goat's milk
200 ml (7 fl oz) thin (pouring) cream
30 g (1 oz) organic roasted unhulled tahini
40 g (1½ oz) honey
6 egg yolks
100 g (3½ oz) caster (superfine) sugar

Slowly warm the milk and cream in a saucepan until it comes to a bare simmer. Add the tahini and honey and stir until melted.

Lightly whisk the egg yolks and sugar. Add to the milk mixture and stir over medium heat until the mixture coats the back of a spoon (83°C/181°F on a sugar thermometer).

Pass the mixture through a fine sieve, into a clean bowl, and place over ice. Stir occasionally until cool.

Now churn the mixture in your ice-cream machine, as per the manufacturer's instructions.

The ice cream will keep in the freezer for up to 4 weeks.

On one ice-cream pilgrimage we made it to the legendary Humphry Slocombe store in San Francisco, where the 'POG' (passionfruit, orange and guava) sorbet was a smash hit. Back home, I thought we'd try a remake. Patrons were starting to love the ice cream that we'd recreated, but we never felt we 'owned' it and had simply borrowed it from hallowed halls. Then we chanced upon an ice cream made with a ricotta-style cheese called requesón. Slam the two together, and finally something to call our own.

MAKES ABOUT 1.25 LITRES (44 FL OZ/5 CUPS)

REQUISITION OF POG

REQUESÓN

1 litre (35 fl oz/4 cups) milk
juice of ½ a lemon
grated zest and juice of ½ an orange

To make the 'kissing second-cousin' of ricotta, scald the milk in a heavy-based saucepan over medium heat.

When the milk is about to boil, quickly add the lemon and orange juices and stir. The milk will start to curdle.

After a couple of minutes, line a colander with some muslin (cheesecloth) and place in the sink, then pour in the cheese. Leave to drain for 20 minutes, before placing the solids in a bowl and stirring through the orange zest and a pinch of salt.

Scoop into a sealable container and place in the fridge until needed. Any left-over cheese will keep for up to 1 week.

POG SORBET

180 ml (6 fl oz) milk
100 ml (3½ fl oz) thin (pouring) cream
100 g (3½ oz) dextrose monohydrate
40 g (1½ oz) caster (superfine) sugar
75 g (2½ oz) skim milk powder
5 g (⅛ oz) gelatine sheets
250 ml (9 fl oz/1 cup) passionfruit juice
250 ml (9 fl oz/1 cup) guava purée
100 g (3½ oz) requesón (see left)

Place the milk and cream in a heavy-based saucepan and gently bring to a bare simmer.

Combine the dextrose, sugar and milk powder, then whisk into the milk mixture.

Soak the gelatine in cold water for 5 minutes, or until soft and pliable. Remove from the water and squeeze out the excess liquid. Add to the pan and stir until dissolved.

Pour the mixture into a bowl, then cool in the fridge. Once cooled, add the passionfruit juice, guava purée and requesón. Use a stick blender to purée until smooth.

Pour into your ice-cream machine, then churn as per the manufacturer's instructions.

The ice cream will keep in the freezer for up to 4 weeks.

What was tutti frutti before it became a concoction, created by an industrial flavour lab, that could strip the paint off a freshly painted car? The seemingly poorly matched flavours in this sorbet make for some interesting reactions. Nobody picks the flavour combo — it's our own little version of tutti fruitiness.

MAKES 500 ML (17 FL OZ/2 CUPS)

BANANA CASSIS SORBET

100 g (3½ oz) fresh blackcurrants
100 g (3½ oz) banana, roughly chopped
90 g (3¼ oz) caster (superfine) sugar
25 g (1 oz) dextrose monohydrate
5 g (⅛ oz) gelatine sheets

Put the blackcurrants and banana in a saucepan with 200 ml (7 fl oz) of water and bring to a simmer. Cook for 10 minutes, or until the fruit is tender. Use a stick blender to blend the mixture until smooth; if there are still too many lumps, pass the mixture through a fine sieve into a bowl, forcing as many solids as possible through the sieve with the back of a ladle.

Combine the sugar and dextrose and add to the purée.

Soak the gelatine in cold water for 5 minutes, or until soft and pliable. Remove the gelatine from the water and squeeze out any excess liquid.

Make sure the fruit purée is warm; if it isn't, warm it for a moment, then add the gelatine and stir to dissolve.

Cool the sorbet in a bowl set over ice, before churning in your ice-cream machine, as per the manufacturer's instructions.

The sorbet will keep in the freezer for up to 4 weeks.

SWEET BIG BESSIE

WE ALL HAVE A DREAM... well, mine was to one day get an ice-cream truck. We were late adopters of the smart phone and social media, but with the smart phone comes 24/7 access to eBay, which for a long while became my strange addiction.

I stumbled upon a Commer Karrier, swinging a price tag of $80,000, so my dream seemed about as likely as winning Lotto. Commer Karriers are the real deal, with beautiful snub-front noses, wide grills and Morris looks — plus these trucks were the original Mr Whippy vans.

With prolonged pig-headedness, I searched on. After two years, another van came up for auction in Perth, Western Australia, so I called the number, but to no avail. The auction ended with no purchase and the van was not relisted, yet the phone line remained dead. Every week I called that number, hoping something would come of my cries down the line. Three months later, voilà: there was a slight English twang in the voice at the end of the line, and after a little wrangling the deal was done. Teena scowled as once again I emptied the bank account, on a blind-buy ice-cream van on the other side of the country.

Teena is the big guns. If you ever thought that something could not happen, send Teena in and BAM! Sorted. Somehow, the van was on its way, even if the final payment was made with only minutes to spare.

Marc, our transport guru, later rang to say the van was ready to collect. She was parked only a few suburbs away, and off I went to get her. There she sat in the yard, diminished, in faded pastel-pink paint and rims that looked like they were purchased from Satan's shopping mall. Marc fixed me with a boyish grin and raised eyebrow, wondering if I had any idea of the project we had just taken on.

Once I finally found a gear, I drove her along the highway. Hmmm, spongy brakes and no clutch... let's just say I have never pumped a set of brakes so hard. Somehow I got her back to the shop without squashing anyone, but I was a quivering mess. I had to explain to Teena that the truck was HUGE! A freaking big Bessie — not the cutesie little truck we were thinking — and practically undriveable. It was a truly butt-clenching moment but Teena, as always, could see the potential of our new girl. For the next few months Bessie sat in the car park as we contacted all the vagabonds and pirates we could muster to fix the clutch, rebuild the gearbox, have her resprayed and get her registered and back on the road.

Bessie's name had stuck, but when I googled 'Big Bessie' a world of warcraft loading pages came up with a truly voluptuous lady who looked a little skanky. We went to our graphic designer Cathy, who has always 'got' our quirky style, and two weeks later I nearly cried: with a few little tweaks her design for Big Bessie was perfect.

Then I read in *Gourmet Traveller* that one of the super pastry chefs of the 'big island' was also about to start an ice-cream truck. I panicked: I am not nearly as talented or good-looking, so what would I do? Yep, one-upmanship: I would make a giant melted ice-cream cone for the top of the truck. After several attempts, we were finally happy with our foam and fibreglass creation, and mounted the cone phallically on top of the truck as a raised finger towards those who would take us on. Ironically, those talked-about pastry dudes never did set up their ice-cream truck...

We were accepted into our first festival with the big fish. The week-long summer 'Taste' festival on the Hobart waterfront is massive and known to turn ill-prepared punters into trembling wrecks. I wanted to make soft-serve ice cream from scratch, and started with the Penn State Prison formula. Ah I nearly cried: the barrel of our ice-cream machine froze solid! I called in the one man who knew our original Van l Carpigiani machine, Laurie Rossiter (aka Mr Fluffy the ice-cream pirate). Laurie zigged, Laurie zagged, cogs were re-shimmed, micro-switches replaced and springs resprung. Three days before the festival, Laurie declared the machine ready.

The council came to give Bessie her final inspection. As we stood in the truck and got the tick, a beeping delivery van reversed up the shop's driveway... Teena screamed and I cringed as the fool backed into Bessie. We jumped out of the truck: one of the quarter panels looked like the apocalypse!

There was not enough time to get Bessie fixed, but Teena had an epiphany — a band-aid solution. She raced home and printed out band-aids, laminated them and stuck them over the damage. We rolled Big Bessie into the festival, our heathen sundaes took off, and our moment of ice-cream redemption had finally come.

Bessie is that point of difference and a chance to let the mind wonder: will people eat a fat Elvis sundae, bacon marmalade... or can I make them think that this ice cream is a contraband drug, name it after a dead celebrity or TV show, float it in booze and sprinkle it with sherbet...

We love our big girl. Next project, Harriett!

Please...
DON'T LICK
THE TRUCK

Sweet Envy's
BIG BESSIE
Soft serves · HARD CHOICES!
GET YOUR cheeky nibbles!
Made with FLAMING PASSION
ICE-CREAM VAN PARKING ONLY
Best Dessert
TASTE
WORLD'S GRANDEST
Ice-cream
SUNDAE ? $10
AMY WINEHOUSE
BOURBON CARAMEL, BROWNIE, CHOC MALT, PEANUTS & SHERBET
SAM I AM
GOOSEBERRY & STRAWBERRY COMPOTE MILK CRUMB, BEVOO & SALT
BEAUTIFUL BURGESS
ROAST NECTARINE, BURNT WHITE CHOC & SALTY WALNUTS
HOT FROZEN DOG
BRIOCHE BUN, SOFT SERVE & HOT SAUCE

"We rolled Big Bessie into the festival, our heathen sundaes took off, and our moment of ice-cream redemption had finally come."

The legendary Big Gay Ice-cream truck in New York sells an amazing range of soft-serve goodness. This is our homage to those greats and their irreverent humour. In Australia, just about every child remembers eating Honey Joys — those clumps of sticky goodness that came nestled in paper cases at Granny's when we were young. This scattering of crispy cornflakes and honey caramel can transport you through time and space. Trust me, it does not get much better than this.

MAKES ENOUGH STICKY BITS FOR 6 ADULTS, OR 1 CHILD

JOY'S PRICKLY BOX

HONEY CARAMEL

210 g (7½ oz) prickly box honey, or other mildly fragrant honey
20 g (¾ oz) butter
150 ml (5 fl oz) thin (pouring) cream

TO ASSEMBLE

vanilla ice cream, to serve
½ quantity of CFC (page 224)
6 waffle cones (optional)

Cook the honey in a medium-sized, heavy-based saucepan over medium heat for 5–10 minutes, or until the honey begins to caramelise and foam up the sides of the pan.

Add the butter. Using a long-handled spoon, stir to deglaze the pan, taking care as the hot mixture may spit.

Remove from the heat and whisk in the cream. Pour the caramel into a heatproof dish.

Now decide whether to serve the sundae hot, or wait the excruciatingly long time to cool the caramel.

This sundae is as easy as it gets. Just scatter the ice cream with the CFC and dredge it in as much honey caramel as you can handle.

It can even be served in a cone, built on top of some scoops of ice cream.

Sometimes stuff just riles me and I feel like rebelling against the trend. Like those freaking tacos I see everywhere now, that are so inauthentic and way removed from anything remotely resembling an essential South American food group. Yep, even in our small country town, the Mexican wave has swallowed the hipsters in its urban tsunami, leaving swathes of punters drooling for their next taco hit. Well, taco freaks, get this one into ya!

MAKES 6 'EL ZOMBIE DE LAS MUERTES'!

TACONE

5 egg yolks
80 g (2¾ oz) caster (superfine) sugar
3 egg whites
75 g (2½ oz) plain (all-purpose) flour
a pinch of sea salt
icing (confectioners') sugar, for dusting
ice cream, to serve
hot sauce of your liking, such as our raspberry sriracha (see the hot frozen dogs recipe on page 215), to serve

Preheat the oven to 190°C (375°F/Gas 5). Line two large baking trays with baking paper.

Using a pencil, trace around the bottom of a saucer or a side plate six times on the baking paper. Flip the paper over and set aside.

In a bowl, whisk the egg yolks and half the caster sugar by hand until pale and creamy. Simultaneously, using a stand mixer, whisk the egg whites to stiff peaks, before adding the remaining caster sugar to make a smooth and shiny meringue.

Fold the meringue into the egg yolks a few additions at a time. Now carefully and gently fold in the flour and salt.

Using a piping (icing) bag fitted with a 7 mm (⅜ inch) nozzle (or just cut the same-sized hole into the end of a disposable piping bag), pipe the sponge mixture in concentric circles onto the paper-lined trays.

Bake for 8 minutes, or until just cooked and light brown.

Slip the sponges onto a cooling rack. Leave until cool enough to handle, then dust with icing sugar.

Hold a sponge in your hand and add some scoops of ice cream. Drizzle with some saucy bits of your choice and devour straight away.

Two of our friends, Roger and Sue, happen to be food critics/writers. While this was daunting at first, as always familiarity breeds contempt (not really!), and I started on a silent mission to get them to eat 'industrial' food. After all, even processed food must once have been as pure as the driven snow. So, here's our take on a mass-produced pop classic. We top the tarts with some lemon icing and a sprinkling of salt, but they are great as they are. And even better with ice cream — definitely part of a complete breakfast!

MAKES 8

TOASTER TARTS

ABBA ZABBA FILLING

6 apples
50 g (1¾ oz) butter
100 g (3½ oz) liquorice, chopped

Peel the apples and begin to sauté in a frying pan with the butter over medium heat. After about 5 minutes, once you get some caramelisation, add the liquorice and continue to cook until the apples are tender.

Give the apples and liquorice a quick whiz in a blender until smooth, then place in the fridge to cool.

FOR THE TARTS

1 quantity of savoury shortcrust pastry (page 227)

Preheat the oven to 180°C (350°F/Gas 4). Roll out the pastry to 2 mm (1⁄16 inch) thick. Cut it into 16 rectangles, measuring about 10 x 15 cm (4 x 6 inches).

Pipe a thin layer of the abba zabba filling onto the eight pastry rectangles, leaving a 1 cm (½ inch) border at the edge. Top each with another pastry rectangle.

Bake the tarts for 15 minutes, until pale golden. Remove from the oven and leave to cool; the tarts can be baked a day ahead.

LEMON ICING

50 ml (1½ fl oz) lemon juice
250 g (9 oz) icing (confectioners') sugar
a pinch of sea salt, for sprinkling

Get everything ready to make the lemon icing, but prepare the icing just before toasting the pop tarts.

Pour the lemon juice into a microwave-proof dish. Zap it in the microwave for 15 seconds so it comes to the boil.

Remove from the microwave, then add the sugar and the salt. Beat until smooth, then use immediately.

TO ASSEMBLE

sea salt, for sprinkling
ice cream, to serve

Give the tarts a quick blast in the toaster, as you would for toast.

Top the tarts with some lemon icing and a sprinkling of salt. Serve with ice cream.

'Burgo' (Luke Burgess) is a too-talented, too-good-looking, way-too-popular chef and friend. The ladies swoon at a mere glance into his flirtatious eyes and stand dumbfounded at his boyish good looks. How the hell can anyone else compete? Mate, here is your sundae — it's beautiful.

MAKES ENOUGH FOR 8 SUNDAES

BEAUTIFUL BURGESS

BURNT WHITE CHOCOLATE

500 g (1 lb 2 oz) white chocolate, roughly chopped

Preheat the oven to 120°C (235°F/Gas ½). Line a baking tray with baking paper and place the chocolate in an even layer across it.

Bake for about 1 hour, using a spatula to move the chocolate around every 10 minutes or so. The chocolate will melt and then seize into a solid lump – don't hold back, just keep baking it until it is good and brown, like the delicious bits of cookies that get slightly burnt in the oven.

Remove from the oven and leave to cool, before chopping into small chunks.

The burnt chocolate can be stored in an airtight container for up to 1 week.

PEACH COMPOTE

8 peaches
50 g (1¾ oz) caster (superfine) sugar
1 lemongrass stem, white part only, lightly bruised with the back of a knife

Cut the peaches into chunks and remove the stones. Put the sugar in a medium-sized saucepan over medium heat and wait for it to caramelise. This will take about 5 minutes.

Add the peach chunks all at once. Slip in the lemongrass and cook for about 5 minutes, or until the peach is tender. Pour into a container and chill in the fridge until needed.

The compote can be made 1–2 days ahead. Remove the lemongrass before using.

TO ASSEMBLE

ice cream, to serve
1 quantity of salted caramelised nuts (page 224), made using walnuts

Serve the ice cream with the peach compote and burnt white chocolate bits and salty walnuts spooned over the top. Perfect.

Best eaten in a stripy T-shirt and skinny jeans.

We've added some extra bits to Sam's Sundae from San Francisco's Bi-Rite Creamery. Our version is not quite right and slightly wrong: we think it may well be Dr Seuss-inspired, and matches perfectly with a meal of green eggs and ham.

MAKES 8 SUNDAES

SAM I AM

I WISH I WERE A TIM TAM

100 g (3½ oz) butter
a pinch of sea salt
40 g (1½ oz) icing (confectioners') sugar
100 g (3½ oz) plain (all-purpose) flour
100 g (3½ oz) white chocolate, chopped
60 g (2¼ oz) milk powder

Preheat the oven to 150°C (300°F/Gas 2). In a bowl, rub together the butter, salt, icing sugar and flour until you get a smooth shortbread dough.

Place the shortbread on a baking tray in random lumps about the size of a small fist. Bake for 15–20 minutes, or until an even golden brown. Remove from the oven and leave to cool.

Melt the chocolate in a heatproof bowl set over a saucepan of simmering water, ensuring the base of the bowl doesn't touch the water.

Break up any large lumps of shortbread, then add the shortbread to the chocolate, mixing lightly.

Add the milk powder and gently stir. Scatter over a baking tray lined with baking paper.

Cool and store in an airtight container for up to 1 week.

BEVOO

1 drop of bergamot essential oil
100 ml (3½ fl oz) extra virgin olive oil

Add the bergamot essential oil to the olive oil and leave to infuse until required.

ELDERFLOWER, GOOSEBERRY & STRAWBERRY COMPOTE

200 g (7 oz) fresh strawberries, hulled
200 g (7 oz) fresh gooseberries, hulled
60 ml (2 fl oz/¼ cup) elderflower cordial

Cut the strawberries in half and place in a saucepan. Add the gooseberries and cordial and cook over medium heat for about 5 minutes, or until the fruit is tender.

Transfer to a container and chill in the fridge until required.

TO ASSEMBLE

ice cream, to serve
sea salt, for sprinkling

For each serve, take a few scoops of ice cream and top with a ladleful of the fruit compote. Sprinkle with I wish I were a Tim Tam, then finish with a sprinkling of sea salt and a swirl of bevoo.

Freaks, this is it. No fancy footwork to introduce this one: it's simply the best sundae we have ever made. It came about by chance, as if by divine miracle, and at some point will count towards our sainthood.

MAKES 8 SUNDAES

AMY WINEHOUSE

CHOCOLATE MALT SAUCE

100 ml (3½ fl oz) milk
250 ml (9 fl oz/1 cup) thin (pouring) cream
50 ml (1¾ fl oz) liquid malt
150 g (5½ oz) dark chocolate, chopped

Pour the milk, cream and malt into a saucepan. Add a pinch of sea salt and bring to the boil.

Put the chocolate in a heatproof bowl. Pour the hot cream mixture over the chocolate and whisk until smooth and lump free.

The sauce will keep in an airtight container for up to 2 weeks.

SHERBET

½ teaspoon citric acid
½ teaspoon cream of tartar
½ teaspoon bicarbonate of soda (baking soda)
120 g (4¼ oz) icing (confectioners') sugar
50 g (1¾ oz) jelly crystals, in a flavour of your choice (try mango or port wine)

Place all the ingredients in a blender and whizz to evenly distribute, or pass the mixture through a fine sieve a few times.

TO ASSEMBLE

ice cream, to serve
½ quantity of salty caramel (page 220), with 60 ml (2 fl oz/¼ cup) bourbon added
½ quantity of brownies (from the chunky monkey recipe on page 168), cut into bite-sized chunks
200 g (7 oz) roasted salted peanuts

For each serve, take a large scoop of ice cream and top it with a large spoonful of chocolate malt sauce, then a large spoonful of salty caramel sauce.

Sprinkle with a large handful of brownie chunks and peanuts, then top with a large spoonful of sherbet powder.

Think large!

JACK & THE
ROOM BOYS

"We needed, wanted, to recreate the fried ice cream of Chinatown, but didn't want to carry around a deep-fryer in our ice-cream truck."

Teena's mum and dad used to run a pub as far south in Tasmania as you can go, and had procured an old hot-dog toaster — the kind you'd find in your old corner store. We tried toasting some brioche on the spit, but the bread would split and our 'hot dog' more closely resembled the *Titanic* than food. So we changed to a milk roll, which allows you to toast the centre perfectly without the whole thing falling apart, and also works mighty fine with an egg and cress filling. Sorry, getting a little side-tracked. Back to that hot frozen dog...

MAKES 8 PORTIONS OF UNHOLY GOODNESS

HOT FROZEN DOGS

HOT DOG BUNS

500 g (1 lb 2 oz) strong flour
1 egg
2 teaspoons sea salt
20 g (¾ oz) caster (superfine) sugar
30 g (1 oz) fresh yeast, or 15 g (½ oz) active dried yeast
20 g (¾ oz) butter
250 ml (9 fl oz/1 cup) milk, plus extra for brushing

Place all the ingredients in the mixing bowl of an electric mixer fitted with a dough hook. Mix for 2 minutes on low speed, then for 6 minutes on medium speed, or until the dough is smooth, shiny and elastic.

Cover and leave to prove in the bowl for 10 minutes.

Divide the dough into eight portions. Mould each into a cigar shape about 12 cm (4½ inches) long. Leave to prove on a baking tray for about 40 minutes, or until doubled in size.

RASPBERRY SRIRACHA

125 g (4½ oz) punnet fresh raspberries
1 tablespoon sugar
2 tablespoons sriracha sauce

Mash all the ingredients together and let the raspberries steep in their own juices for a good few hours.

You can make the sauce smooth by giving it a whiz with a stick blender, but I quite like a slightly lumpy feel.

TO ASSEMBLE

ice cream, to serve

Preheat the oven to 200°C (400°C/Gas 6). Brush the rolls with a little milk, then bake for 15 minutes, or until a light golden brown.

Remove the rolls from the oven. Leave to cool slightly, then cut in half.

Now lightly toast in the oven, cut side up, until golden and slightly crisp – or if, like us, you are lucky enough to have a hot dog machine, toast the buns in this.

Fill with ice cream, then drizzle with raspberry sriracha to keep it real.

Serve hot, in paper napkins.

Our Mother recipes are a part of our shop's DNA — the things we come back to again and again, like family. Reliable, comforting and amazing, they form the building blocks of bigger and better things.

THE MOTHER RECIPES

Christina Tosi, of Momofuku Milk Bar fame, has her 'mother dough' — one dough recipe that gets used in a whole bunch of ways at this iconic New York bakery.

Pondering on Christina's revelatory cookbook *Milk*, we began to realise just how often some base recipes repeat within our own shop.

For me, Christina's evocative description of her 'mother dough' stirred up childhood memories of Mum's large maroon, cocoa-powder-stained diary, filled with precious recipes like Aunty Peggy's rice dish and apple 'novel' pudding. The diary is a sacred holy file that, if the house were on fire, I swear would be grabbed first.

There is something tactile about keeping your favourite recipes in a book that you can call on when in need of a sure thing. Such books hold a certain place in time, as if captured, waiting to unleash their magic upon those who find them.

These are our own 'Mother' recipes, the ones that link the shop together: essential cakes and crispy and gooey bits that can be mixed, smeared and smudged into all manner of combinations.

Our Mother recipes are a part of our shop's DNA — the things we come back to again and again, like family. Reliable, comforting and amazing, they form the building blocks of bigger and better things.

SALTY CARAMEL

MAKES THREE 400 ML (14 FL OZ) JARS

There isn't a cook worth their salt who doesn't have a good salty caramel recipe. Eternally popular, it manages to find its way into nearly all of the best-sellers in our shop, and becomes even more transcendent when paired with ice cream. Always make lots so you can give some to your best friends as gifts, or store in jars for some late-night resplendent pleasure.

400 g (14 oz) caster (superfine) sugar
160 g (5½ oz) liquid glucose
60 g (2¼ oz) butter
10 g (¼ oz) sea salt
600 ml (21 fl oz) thin (pouring) cream

Place the sugar and glucose in a large heavy-based saucepan over medium heat. (A bigger saucepan is better, as the caramel is prone to spitting.) Cook, stirring occasionally, until the sugar has dissolved. Now increase the heat and cook until the caramel is a dark amber colour.

Once you have your desired colour, deglaze the pan by carefully stirring in the butter and salt, to slow down the colour progression. (Beware, this caramel likes to spit molten blobs of lava at you.)

Remove the pan from the heat. Using a long-handled spoon, carefully add the cream in a few additions, standing back to avoid hot caramel splatters.

Leave the caramel in the pan overnight, or pour into sterilised heatproof jars and leave to cool.

The salty caramel will keep in the pantry for 2–3 weeks.

CAJETA

MAKES TWO 400 ML (14 FL OZ) JARS

This welcome addition to the caramel family comes from South America. When you can get fresh goat's milk, it takes on a life of its own, and has an understated savoury 'umami' flavour that is hard to emulate.

500 ml (17 fl oz/2 cups) goat's milk
250 g (9 oz) caster (superfine) sugar
½ teaspoon sea salt
½ teaspoon bicarbonate of soda (baking soda)

Place all the goodness in a large saucepan and bring to a simmer. Be sure to simmer the mixture slowly, avoiding the desire to turn the heat up and fill your house with burnt goat smells.

Now slowly simmer the mixture for a good 1–1½ hours, until it reaches 108°C (226°F) on a sugar thermometer – or do your granny proud and test the set by dropping small blobs on a chilled saucer, until you're happy with the consistency.

Pour into sterilised heatproof jars and leave to cool. The cajeta will keep in the pantry for 2–3 weeks.

It is delicious over ice cream, smeared atop waffles, but best of all, for dipping churros in.

LEMON CURD

MAKES TWO 400 ML (14 FL OZ) JARS

This method of making lemon curd may seem a little abstract, but the beauty is that by aerating the curd, it is much lighter and less cloying than other lemon curds. We started making lemon curd in London, where it appeased the savage beasties, and have never looked back. At the shop we use this same method but change the flavours, from passionfruit and tonka bean, to basil and lime.

3 eggs
175 g (6 oz) caster (superfine) sugar
grated zest and juice of 2 lemons (you'll need about 100 ml/3½ fl oz of juice)
275 g (9¾ oz) butter, at room temperature
5 g (⅛ oz) gelatine sheets

Using electric beaters, whisk the eggs and sugar in a heatproof bowl until light and fluffy, as you would for a classic sponge cake.

Place the bowl over a saucepan of gently simmering water, ensuring the base of the bowl doesn't touch the water. Add the lemon zest and juice, occasionally whisking gently until the mixture reaches 83°C/181°F on a sugar thermometer (it should coat the back of a spoon).

Set aside to cool to 50°C/122°F, then stir in the butter (make sure it's at room temperature).

Soak the gelatine in a bowl of cold water for 5 minutes. Drain and squeeze out the excess liquid. Add the gelatine to the lemon mixture while the mixture is still warm. Stir to ensure all the gelatine has completely dissolved.

Pour into sterilised jars, then cool and place in the fridge overnight. The lemon curd will keep in the fridge for up to 2 weeks.

CARROT MARMALADE

MAKES TWO 400 ML (14 FL OZ) JARS

Jess, a young barista lass, took the challenge to come over to the dark side, and made us some of this marmalade that was much loved at the coffee house she worked at in London. I feel it's a light version of the usual heavy-hitting English preserve: think of it as marmalade on training wheels. When it comes to cooking this marmalade, it's more of a reduction than a classic jam or preserve. And it gets 'dude' points because of its seemingly random vegetable inclusion! Meyer lemons, if you can get them, will give the marmalade a lovely light, perfumed flavour.

500 g (1 lb 2 oz) carrots
2 Meyer lemons, washed well
350 g (12 oz) caster (superfine) sugar

Pour plenty of water into a saucepan and bring to a simmer. Peel the carrots, then blanch them in the simmering water for 10 minutes, or until tender; they can still be a little on the firm side. Drain, then set aside to cool.

Grate the carrots and lemons quite coarsely, keeping the skin on the lemons.

Throw all the ingredients in a saucepan and bring to the boil. Reduce the heat and simmer for 30 minutes, or until a good jammy consistency is achieved.

Transfer to sterilised heatproof jars and use as needed. The marmalade will keep in the pantry for several months.

BANANA JAM

MAKES TWO 400 ML (14 FL OZ) JARS

Sometimes you need a simple banana number that will not oxidise and turn brown when exposed to air, and doesn't require half a chemistry lab to achieve. This is our banana superstar.

200 g (7 oz) caster (superfine) sugar
2 bananas, diced
15 ml (½ fl oz) liquid malt

Place the sugar in a heavy-based saucepan over medium heat. Stir occasionally until the sugar has dissolved, turns a deep caramel colour and begins to foam.

Add half the diced banana and stir until there are no lumps of caramel, then follow with the remaining banana and the liquid malt.

Allow the jam to cool in the pan, then transfer to sterilised jars.

Store in the fridge until needed. The jam will keep for about 2 weeks.

BACON MARMALADE

MAKES TWO 400 ML (14 FL OZ) JARS

I have a firm belief that pork can make everything a little better. Living in Tasmania, there is always someone willing to trade services for a porcine delight. This bacon marmalade was born out of a slight overabundance of all things good, with an upcoming festival where we thought we'd shake up the locals with lashings of crispy pork scattered over bowls of sumptuous ice cream. The wonderful counterplay of pig, smoke, hot, sweet and sour reminds me of a backstreet Thai food truck, which makes me feel a little dirty, and I like it.

250 g (9 oz) cured and smoked bacon, coarsely ground (minced)
1 brown onion, diced
1 garlic bulb, cloves diced
70 g (2½ oz) dark brown sugar
60 ml (2 fl oz/¼ cup) bourbon
50 ml (1½ fl oz) maple syrup
50 ml (1½ fl oz) sriracha sauce
40 g (1½ oz) tamarind purée
50 ml (1½ fl oz) soy sauce
pinch of freshly ground black pepper

Put the bacon in a large frying pan over medium heat. Cook for about 10 minutes to render the fat from the bacon. Add the onion and garlic.

After about 10 minutes, once the onion is nicely caramelised, add the remaining ingredients and cook over low heat for about 30 minutes, or until the sauce has reduced and begins to stick to the bacon.

Leave to cool, then transfer to sterilised jars. Now go out into the world and find yourself a victim.

The marmalade will keep in the fridge for up to 1 week. Serve at room temperature.

CARAMELISED NUTS

MAKES ABOUT 200 G (7 OZ)

No real need to introduce this with random words of suspect philosophical motivation. It's really quite obvious: caramelised nuts just taste better.

150 g (5½ oz) caster (superfine) sugar
200 g (7 oz) nuts of your choice (choose one, or all!)
sea salt, for sprinkling (optional)

Place the sugar and 150 ml (5 fl oz) of water in a medium saucepan and bring to the boil. Add the nuts and let steep while you warm the oven up to a balmy 160°C (315°C/Gas 2-3).

Line a baking tray with baking paper. Drain the nuts and place on the baking tray. Sprinkle with a little salt if it's your thing, then bake for about 10 minutes.

Remove from the oven and leave to cool before using. The nuts will keep in an airtight container for several months.

CFC

FILLS ABOUT THREE 400 ML (14 FL OZ) JARS

CFC = Corn Flake Crispy, great for adding to a whole bunch of dishes where a little crunch is needed. To own a little of this space and keep it iconically Australian, we went with the Honey Joys theme (an after-school treat in which Cornflakes are doused in honey and baked in paper cases), using our favourite local honey, Tasmanian prickly box.

150 g (5½ oz) butter
50 g (1¾ oz) prickly box honey, or other mildly fragrant honey
70 g (2½ oz) caster (superfine) sugar
200 g (7 oz) cornflakes

Preheat the oven to 170°C (325°C/Gas 3). Line a baking tray with baking paper.

Put the butter, honey and sugar in a saucepan over medium heat. Stir gently until the sugar dissolves; you can check by rubbing a little mixture between your fingers, feeling for the sugar grains.

Place the cornflakes in a bowl, add the honey mixture and toss until thoroughly coated.

Spread on the baking tray and bake for about 15 minutes, or until the flakes are a dark golden colour, moving them around a few times with a spatula, to stop the outside edges burning.

Remove from the oven and cool on the tray, before placing in airtight containers. The CFC will keep in the pantry for 2–3 weeks.

NEVER-FAIL PASTRY CREAM

MAKES ABOUT 750 G (1 LB 10 OZ)

Chef Neil Ferguson gave me this recipe in London. It always makes the best soufflés and never gets any lumps. Nowadays, we use this old soufflé base as pastry cream/custard/crème pâtissière wherever we need it.

460 ml (16¼ fl oz) milk
1 vanilla bean, cut in half lengthways, seeds scraped
95 g (3½ oz) caster (superfine) sugar
70 g (2½ oz) plain (all-purpose) flour
50 g (1¾ oz) butter
3 egg yolks

Put the milk in a saucepan with the vanilla bean and seeds, and 25 g (1 oz) of the sugar. Bring to a simmer.

Rub together the flour, butter and the remaining 70 g (2½ oz) of sugar until the mixture resembles fine crumbs.

Once the milk has come to the boil, remove the vanilla bean. Tip in the flour mixture all at once and cook, stirring, until there is no residual flour flavour. This will probably take about 5 minutes.

Pour the mixture into the bowl of a stand mixer and begin whisking at low speed. Add the egg yolks and keep mixing until cool. This will probably take about 10 minutes.

Transfer to an airtight container. The pastry cream will keep in the fridge for up to 3 days.

SWEET PASTRY

MAKES ENOUGH FOR ONE 20–25 CM (8–10 INCH) TART, OR A DOZEN 10 CM (4 INCH) TARTS

This versatile pastry is one of the building blocks of good baking. It can be used for tarts, pies and all manner of biscuits.

400 g (14 oz) pastry flour
120 g (4¼ oz) icing (confectioners') sugar
240 g (8½ oz) butter
a pinch of sea salt
1 egg

In a bowl, rub together the flour, icing sugar, butter and salt until the mixture resembles fine crumbs.

Add the egg and mix as little as possible to bring the dough together.

Divide into two or three manageable portions and wrap in plastic wrap. Rest the dough in the fridge for at least a few hours before using. The pastry can be made up to 2 days ahead.

CHOCOLATE SWEET PASTRY

Prepare as above, using 325 g (11½ oz) of pastry flour instead of 400 g (14 oz), and adding 75 g (2½ oz) of sifted Dutch-processed cocoa powder with the flour and icing sugar.

PUFF PASTRY

MAKES ENOUGH FOR TWO 22 CM (8½ INCH) PIES, OR A DOZEN 10 CM (4 INCH) PIES

Puff pastry had always been the bane of my existence until I stole this recipe. The irony is that my pastry-making skills probably have not improved that much, but now I take myself a whole lot less seriously! Full butter puff pastry just cannot be beaten, and once made and turned you can freeze it in pie-sized lumps, ready for easy execution at a moment's notice. Never throw away any scraps of puff pastry when you're making sausage rolls, pies or whatever. Stack the scraps on top of each other, then wrap them in plastic wrap and keep in the freezer, so you can pull the pastry out when you need it.

100 g (3½ oz) butter, plus 700 g (1 lb 9 oz) cold butter
1 kg (2 lb 4 oz) strong flour
400 ml (14 fl oz) milk
100 ml (3½ fl oz) thin (pouring) cream
20 g (¾ oz) sea salt

Place the 100 g (3½ oz) of butter in a small saucepan. Cook for 5 minutes over medium heat, or until nut brown. Leave to cool.

Pour the browned butter into the bowl of a stand mixer. Add the flour, milk, cream and salt. Using the pastry-mixing attachment, mix to a firm dough. Wrap the dough in plastic wrap and chill in the refrigerator overnight.

Pull out the dough and roll into a large square, about 3–4 cm (1¼–1½ inches) thick.

Roll the 700 g (1 lb 9 oz) cold butter into an even sheet about 1 cm (½ inch) thick. Place the sheet of butter on top of the dough, in the centre. Fold the corners of the dough in, as if making an envelope.

Now start to incorporate the butter into the dough, by rolling the dough out into a long strip, about 2–3 cm (¾–1¼ inches) thick. Fold each end of the pastry back into the centre, and then fold one half of the pastry over again. You will now have a square of dough, four layers thick. Turn the dough 90 degrees between each turn, so the dough resembles a book, and the opening is to the right, before repeating the process each time.

You will need to roll and turn the pastry three times in total, and rest the pastry in the fridge for at least 1 hour between each turn.

Do not attempt to speed up the process by shortening the chilling times, or you'll end up with an inferior product.

SAVOURY SHORTCRUST PASTRY

MAKES ENOUGH FOR ONE 25 CM (10 INCH) DEEP-DISH PIE, OR 8–10 INDIVIDUAL 12–15 CM (4½–6 INCH) PIES

Great for savoury pies and quiches, this simple shortcrust is also amazing for making apple pie.

400 g (14 oz) pastry flour
200 g (7 oz) butter
2 teaspoons sea salt
100 ml (3½ fl oz) milk

In a bowl, rub together the flour, butter and salt until the mixture resembles fine crumbs.

Add the milk and mix as little as possible, just enough to bring the dough together.

Divide into two or three manageable portions and wrap in plastic wrap. Rest the dough in the fridge for at least a few hours before using. The pastry can be made up to 2 days ahead.

TRADITIONAL FRUIT CAKE

MAKES ONE 20 CM (8 INCH) ROUND CAKE

This cake is best started at least two or three days in advance to give the flavours a chance to develop. The longer the cake is allowed to mature, the better the flavour will be. We often make ours three to six months ahead, brushing the cake weekly with lashings of rum or brandy. Fruit cakes aren't suitable for cake designs that need to be layered and filled: they are too crumbly and knobbly with fruit to cut into clean layers.

150 g (5½ oz) sultanas (golden raisins)
100 g (3½ oz) raisins
200 g (7 oz) currants
50 g (1¾ oz) glacé cherries
grated zest of 1 lemon
grated zest and juice of 1 orange
25 ml (½ fl oz) brandy
25 ml (½ fl oz) vanilla extract
200 g (7 oz) butter
200 g (7 oz) dark brown sugar
3 eggs
200 g (7 oz) plain (all-purpose) flour
1 teaspoon mixed (pumpkin pie) spice
80 g (2¾ oz) slivered almonds

Place all the dried fruit in a large container. Add the citrus zests and juice, the brandy and vanilla and give it all a good mix. Cover and allow to steep at least overnight, or preferably for 2–3 days, to enhance the flavour.

Preheat the oven to 140°C (275°F/Gas 1). Grease a 20 cm (8 inch) round cake tin and line with baking paper.

Cream the butter and sugar using a stand mixer until pale and creamy. Add the eggs one at a time, beating well each time.

Sift the flour and mixed spice, add to the butter mixture and beat to a smooth batter.

Fold in the soaked fruit and the almonds. Spoon into the lined tin and bake for 3 hours, or until a skewer inserted into the middle of the cake comes out clean. Leave to cool overnight in the tin.

Wrap the cake in waxed paper, then a layer of foil, and store in a cool dry place for at least 2–3 days. It will keep for 3–6 months and benefits from a weekly brushing with rum or brandy. It is best not to freeze an un-iced fruit cake as it will dry out.

VANILLA BUTTER CAKE

MAKES ONE THREE-LAYER 20 CM (8 INCH) ROUND CAKE

This wonderfully buttery classic cake is deliciously innocent in vanilla form, but you can glam it up by adding other flavours to the basic batter (see the suggestions at the end of the recipe). The cake will be easier to cut and layer if made a day ahead.

320 g (11¼ oz) butter
360 g (12¾ oz) sugar
36 g (1¼ oz) liquid glucose (see tip)
5 eggs
540 g (1 lb 3 oz) plain (all-purpose) flour
1 teaspoon salt
25 g (1 oz) baking powder
240 ml (8 fl oz) milk
1 teaspoon vanilla extract

Preheat the oven to 180°C (350°F/Gas 4). Line a 20 cm (8 inch) round cake tin with baking paper.

Using a stand mixer, cream the butter, sugar and glucose until pale and creamy. Add the eggs one at a time, beating well each time.

Sift the flour, salt and baking powder together. Add in batches to the batter, alternating with the milk and vanilla. With each addition, beat until the ingredients are incorporated, but do not overmix or the cake will be tough. Stir in any desired flavour additions (see right).

Smooth into the lined cake tin and bake for 30 minutes, or until a skewer inserted into the middle of the cake comes out clean.

Leave to cool in the tin for 10 minutes, before turning out onto a wire rack to cool completely.

Once cooled, keep in an airtight container in the fridge for up to 2 days, or wrap well and freeze for up to 2 weeks.

To serve, cut the cake horizontally into three equal layers and fill with your choice of filling.

✕ NOT SO STICKY ✕

When measuring liquid glucose, first weigh out the sugar on your digital scales, leave the sugar on the scales and pour the glucose straight over the sugar – saves messing around with the sticky stuff, and there'll be a bit less washing up.

VARIATIONS

lemon cake
Add the grated zest and juice of 3 lemons.
orange cake
Add the grated zest and juice of 2 oranges.
almond cake
Add 50 ml (1½ fl oz) of almond milk.
espresso cake
Add 2 shots of espresso coffee.

CHOCOLATE FUDGE CAKE

MAKES ONE THREE-LAYER 20 CM (8 INCH) ROUND CAKE

We hate mudcake: *fudge* cake sounds far more appealing! This is our version of the modern classic.

5 eggs
650 g (1 lb 7 oz) sugar
250 g (9 oz) butter, melted
150 g (5½ oz) Dutch-processed cocoa powder
360 g (12¾ oz) plain (all-purpose) flour
2 teaspoons baking powder
200 g (7 oz) plain yoghurt
450 ml (16 fl oz) milk

Preheat the oven to 180°C (350°F/Gas 4). Line a 20 cm (8 inch) round cake tin with baking paper.

Using an electric mixer, whisk the eggs, sugar and melted butter until light and fluffy.

Sift the cocoa powder, flour and baking powder together. Combine the yoghurt and milk.

Alternately add the dry ingredients and liquids to the egg mixture in three equal batches. Mix to a smooth silky batter.

Pour into the lined tin and bake for 40 minutes, or until a skewer inserted into the middle of the cake comes out clean.

Leave to cool in the tin for 10 minutes, before turning out onto a wire rack to cool completely.

Once cooled, keep in an airtight container in the fridge for up to 1 week, or wrap well and freeze for 2–3 weeks.

To serve, cut the cake horizontally into three equal layers and fill with your choice of filling.

ROYAL ICING

MAKES ABOUT 350 G (12 OZ)

Royal icing sets very hard and can be used for covering cakes, or for piping intricate designs onto a cake. When preparing the icing, you can colour it to the desired shade by tinting it with a few drops of liquid food colouring, bearing in mind that the icing will darken as it dries. It is best to make royal icing just before using. It is difficult to make the icing in smaller quantities than given here, so if you have any left over, store it in a zip-lock bag at room temperature, rather than the fridge. It separates on standing, but can be whipped to bring it together again.

1 egg white
350 g (12 oz) icing (confectioners') sugar, sifted
juice of ½ a lemon

Place the egg white in a clean, grease-free mixing bowl. Using an electric mixer, whisk to form soft peaks.

Slowly add the sifted icing sugar until incorporated, then mix on high speed until smooth and glossy. Add the lemon juice and mix for another minute.

CREAMY VANILLA FROSTING

MAKES ENOUGH TO FROST ONE 20 CM (8 INCH) ROUND CAKE, OR ABOUT A DOZEN CUPCAKES

This simple vanilla frosting can take on a range of other divine or whimsical flavourings, giving you ample scope to take our basic vanilla butter cake (page 229) or chocolate fudge cake (page 230) in all sorts of fantastical directions.

300 g (10½ oz) butter
250 g (9 oz) icing (confectioners') sugar
100 ml (3½ fl oz) milk
1 vanilla bean, cut in half lengthways, seeds scraped

Set up your stand mixer with the beating attachment and beat the butter and sugar into oblivion – usually for no less than 10 minutes!

Warm the milk and add the vanilla bean pod and seeds. Leave to infuse for 5 minutes, then discard the vanilla bean.

Slowly beat the warm milk into the frosting, being careful not to wear it.

The frosting is now ready to use, although you will probably want to add some extra flavours (see below). For best results use straight away. It can be covered and refrigerated for a few days; pull it out of the fridge a few hours before you plan to use it, and beat the frosting again to soften it.

VARIATIONS

Here are some of the flavours we regularly use. Adjust the proportions to suit your own taste.

caramel frosting
Add 1 tablespoon of salty caramel (page 221).

chocolate frosting
Stir in 2 tablespoons of ganache (right).

orange frosting
Add the finely chopped zest of 1 orange.

lemon frosting
Add the finely chopped zest of 1 lemon.

honey frosting
Stir in 1 tablespoon of honey.

peanut butter frosting
Add 1 tablespoon of peanut butter.

GANACHE

MAKES ENOUGH TO COVER ONE 20 CM (8 INCH) ROUND CAKE

A decadent chocolate frosting and filling. This quantity is easy enough to make as needed, but you can also leave it at room temperature in an airtight container for a few hours or overnight. Stir it smooth again before using.

200 g (7 oz) dark chocolate (70% cocoa)
200 ml (7 fl oz) thin (pouring) cream

Put the chocolate in a heatproof bowl.

Bring the cream to the boil in a small saucepan, then pour the hot cream over the chocolate and leave it alone for 2 minutes.

Use a hand whisk to lightly remove any lumps and emulsify the mixture into a smooth, shiny ganache, without aerating it too much, as you don't want air bubbles.

VARIATION

raspberry dark chocolate
Stir in 1–2 tablespoons raspberry jam.

The simple tips and techniques in the following pages will help you create Teena's amazing cakes in the Cakeatorium chapter. Here you'll find invaluable advice on assembling the cakes, as well as simple charts to help you adapt the recipes for cakes of different shapes and sizes, and ca culate the quantities of sugar paste (rolled fondant), frosting and ganache you'll need for each one.

MOTHER CAKE TRICKS

BASE BOARD AND CAKE BOARDS

We use two different kinds of boards for cake decorating: a base board (also called a cake drum), which the entire finished cake sits on top of, and cake boards (or hard boards).

All the cakes in the Cakeatorium chapter will need a base board.

The base board is quite thick and very sturdy, and for the cakes in this book, needs to be wider than the base of the finished cake. For a professional finish, it is usually covered with a layer of sugar paste (rolled fondant) before the finished cake is placed on top. The base board should be covered with the sugar paste at least a day before it is needed, to allow the sugar paste to set properly, so it isn't deformed by the weight of the cake or cakes on top.

Cake boards or hard boards are slightly thinner than the base board. Their sole function is to provide an invisible means of support between cakes that are stacked on top of each other, so the cakes don't collapse into one another.

Base boards and cake boards are available from cake decorating supply shops.

COVERING THE BASE BOARD

To cover the base board, brush it with cooled boiled water, then roll out your sugar paste to 3 mm (⅛ inch) thick and lay it over the board.

Run your cake smoother over the surface to push out any air pockets. Trim away the excess sugar paste by running a small sharp knife or palette knife around the edge, keeping it flush with the board.

Finish by fastening ribbon trim around the edge, using double-sided tape.

LAYERING AND 'DIRTY ICE'

To fill cakes with frosting or ganache, first cut each cake horizontally into three equal layers, using a sharp knife or cake leveller.

Place the bottom cake layer on a cake board of the same size. Pipe the frosting or ganache over the cake.

Place the next cake layer on top and cover with frosting or ganache.

Place the final cake layer on top. Now give the whole cake a fine coating of frosting or ganache, around the sides and top – this is called 'dirty ice', and helps trap the crumbs so they won't get into the final icing layer; when you dirty-ice, this also gives your final icing something to stick to.

Once you have dirty-iced, allow the frosting or ganache to firm up for about 10 minutes, and the cake is ready to cover.

COVERING A FILLED CAKE WITH SUGAR PASTE

Lightly dust a clean work surface with icing (confectioners') sugar. Knead your sugar paste until it is pliable and smooth.

Evenly roll out the sugar paste about 3–5 mm (1⁄8–1⁄4 inch) thick, and to a size large enough to cover the top and sides of the cake. You can use a piece of string to measure the cake's dimensions, allowing for a little excess.

Lift the sugar paste with a rolling pin, lay it over your cake, then gently push it down the sides. Smooth the top and sides with your hands, carefully pressing the icing against the cake.

Finish by polishing the icing with a cake smoother and trimming away any excess with a sharp knife.

STACKING CAKES ON TOP OF EACH OTHER

When stacking cakes on top of each other, you'll need to use some hidden cake boards and wooden or plastic cake dowels for support, to keep the cakes stable and to stop the top cake tiers sinking into the bottom tier.

All the cakes in the Cakeatorium chapter are stacked centrally, so they sit in the middle of each other; cakes can also be positioned so that one tier is offset to one side or corner.

Once your cakes are covered and ready to stack, push in some dowels, all the way down to the base board, making sure to position the dowels so they'll sit 2.5 cm (1 inch) inside the cake above, spacing them evenly. As a guide, use four dowels for a 20 cm (8 inch) cake, and six dowels for a 30 cm (12 inch) cake.

Now you need to ensure the dowels are all the same length (so the cake above will sit perfectly level). Mark each dowel at the point it surfaces from the cake, remove it from the cake, then line the dowels up on the table to find the average mark. Cut all the dowels (using a sharp knife or other cutting implement) to that same length, to ensure an evenly stable support base for the cake above.

Reinsert the dowels and spread a small amount of royal icing (page 230) in the centre of the cake.

Gently lift the next tier into position. Repeat the process until all the cake tiers are in place.

THE 'BLOCKING' METHOD

You can use hidden foam or polystyrene blocks to support a tiered cake, or to hold a border of flowers or other decorations between the cake tiers.

Place a foam block in the centre of the bottom cake tier and secure in place with royal icing (page 230).

Insert a dowel on each side of the foam block, at the centre point of each edge.

Mark each dowel at the point it touches the top edge of the foam, then remove. Line the dowels up on the table to find the tallest mark, then cut them all to that length to ensure your cake is level.

Reinsert the dowels. Spread a small amount of royal icing on top of the foam block. Gently lift the next cake tier (on its cake board) into position.

Repeat until all the cake tiers are in place.

ADAPTING RECIPES FOR DIFFERENT CAKE SIZES

Some of the tiered cakes in the Cakeatorium chapter use cakes of different sizes. The vanilla butter cake (page 229), chocolate fudge cake (page 230) and traditional fruit cake (page 228) recipes each make a 20 cm (8 inch) round cake.

To make a square or round cake of a different size, use the chart below as a guide to adapt the base cake recipe, remembering that one quantity is based on a 20 cm (8 inch) round cake.

If you need to make a cake smaller than the sizes shown, it is best to reduce the quantity by no more than half, as quantities smaller than this are difficult to mix.

Cooking times are given in each recipe. You will need to increase or decrease the cooking time slightly for each 5 cm (2 inch) variation in cake tin sizes.

ROUND CAKES	SQUARE CAKES	QUANTITY*
15 cm (6 inch)	12.5 cm (5 inch)	½
17.5 cm (7 inch)	15 cm (6 inch)	¾
20 cm (8 inch)	17.5 cm (7 inch)	1
22.5 cm (9 inch)	20 cm (8 inch)	1¼
25 cm (10 inch)	22.5 cm (9 inch)	1½
27.5 cm (11 inch)	25 cm (10 inch)	2
30 cm (12 inch)	27.5 cm (11 inch)	2½
–	30 cm (12 inch)	3

* 1 quantity is based on a 20 cm (8 inch) round cake

SUGAR PASTE QUANTITIES FOR COVERING BASE BOARDS

See below to work out how much sugar paste (rolled fondant) you'll need for covering base boards of different sizes.

ROUND CAKES	SQUARE CAKES	SUGAR PASTE
17.5 cm (7 inch)	–	325 g (11½ oz)
20 cm (8 inch)	17.5 cm (7 inch)	450 g (1 lb)
22.5 cm (9 inch)	20 cm (8 inch)	575 g (1 lb 4½ oz)
25 cm (10 inch)	22.5 cm (9 inch)	700 g (1 lb 9 oz)
27.5 cm (11 inch)	25 cm (10 inch)	825 g (1 lb 13 oz)
30 cm (12 inch)	27.5 cm (11 inch)	950 g (2 lb 2 oz)
35 cm (14 inch)	30 cm (12 inch)	1.2 kg (2 lb 11 oz)
40 cm (16 inch)	35 cm (14 inch)	1.5 kg (3 lb 5 oz)
–	40 cm (16 inch)	1.8 kg (4 lb)

SUGAR PASTE QUANTITIES FOR COVERING CAKES

Here is a guide to how much sugar paste (rolled fondant) you'll need to cover cakes of different shapes and sizes.

ROUND CAKES	SQUARE CAKES	SUGAR PASTE
15 cm (6 inch)	–	750 g (1 lb 10 oz)
17.5 cm (7 inch)	15 cm (6 inch)	850 g (1 lb 14 oz)
20 cm (8 inch)	17.5 cm (7 inch)	1 kg (2 lb 4 oz)
22.5 cm (9 inch)	20 cm (8 inch)	1.25 kg (2 lb 12 oz)
25 cm (10 inch)	22.5 cm (9 inch)	1.5 kg (3 lb 5 oz)
27.5 cm (11 inch)	25 cm (10 inch)	1.8 kg (4 lb)
30 cm (12 inch)	27.5 cm (11 inch)	2.1 kg (4 lb 10 oz)
35 cm (14 inch)	30 cm (12 inch)	2.5 kg (5 lb 8 oz)
–	35 cm (14 inch)	3 kg (6 lb 12 oz)

FROSTING AND GANACHE QUANTITY GUIDE

The creamy vanilla frosting (page 231) and ganache (page 231) recipes are sufficient for filling one 20 cm (8 inch) cake.

To work out how much frosting and ganache you'll need for cakes of other sizes, simply consult the chart below.

ROUND CAKES	SQUARE CAKES	ICING/GANACHE
17.5 cm (7 inch)	–	1 quantity
20 cm (8 inch)	17.5 cm (7 inch)	1 quantity
22.5 cm (9 inch)	20 cm (8 inch)	1 quantity
25 cm (10 inch)	22.5 cm (9 inch)	1½ x quantity
27.5 cm (11 inch)	25 cm (10 inch)	1½ x quantity
30 cm (12 inch)	27.5 cm (11 inch)	1½ x quantity
35 cm (14 inch)	30 cm (12 inch)	2 x quantity
40 cm (16 inch)	35 cm (14 inch)	2 x quantity
–	40 cm (16 inch)	2 x quantity

BACKDOOR FANNY'S

WE LOVE THE PERSONA OF THE late Fanny Craddock, an English television cook, restaurant critic and writer, famous for her acid wit and credited with the invention of the prawn cocktail. In keeping with her tongue-in-cheek ways, one summer we decided we would sell some special treats from the shop's back door under her moniker.

We started our outdoor Backdoor Fanny's food frivolities with a 'ghetto' dessert bar, dishing slap-up treats from Big Bessie, parked at the end of the alley beside our shop. It gave ice-cream addicts a chance to get some sundae action outside of festivals, without having to order our truck around to their place for a quick fix.

Soon enough the tidal wave of burger-eating and young hipsters selling gourmet burgers had spread across the waters to Hobart, but I still felt the burgers kept falling short of those fantastic granulated versions we'd discovered on our pilgrimage to San Francisco. It was time to add a good ground Fanny Burger to Backdoor Fanny's menu!

Our Backdoor Fanny's evenings are not really a money-making venture; the weeks in summer are long, hot and hard, the kitchen is strained to the limit, churning out sheet cake to fill orders for wedding and novelty cakes. It's more about taking a moment, in our own heathen way, to celebrate and hang out with the few and gorge ourselves on burgers and sundaes. It's not really a 'pop up', it's more a 'pop out', as we remove all the furniture from the shop and place it in the void down the side alley.

Hey, everything's better with a bit of Fanny!

There is one dish that will divide as well as unite every chef, cook, backyard hooligan and the like: the burger. This is a burger tribute to the greatest TV food celebrity of all time, Fanny Craddock. We are grinders and admire British Michelin-starred chef Heston Blumenthal's 'granulated' burgers, but hate to see good beef fillet ground up into a burger. No, let's keep in the tasty cuts — the stuff the people eat. Let's not turn the humble burger into some form of egocentric nourishment! This is definitely a commitment burger, as you need to start the preparation one or two days before you actually wish to devour it.

MAKES 8–10 BURGERS

FANNY BURGER

500 g (1 lb 2 oz) beef brisket
500 g (1 lb 2 oz) beef short ribs (ask your butcher to cut the bones out)
500 g (1 lb 2 oz) chuck steak
30 g (1 oz) sea salt
300 g (10½ oz) pork back fat
rendered beef fat, lard or oil, for pan-frying

TO SERVE

caramelised onions
good cheddar cheese
soft burger buns
sauce or ketchup of your choice

Clean all the meat of any gristly bits and reserve any fat. Dice all the meat into 3 cm (1¼ inch) chunks; you can mix the brisket and short rib, but keep the chuck steak separate.

Season the meat with the salt. Place on a cake cooling rack set over a plate and leave uncovered in the fridge for 24–48 hours. This helps dry the meat, concentrating the flavour; the salt also reacts with the proteins in the meat, helping it to clump together.

A good few hours before you want to cook your burgers, chill your meat grinder and meat in the freezer for 30 minutes. (You want everything really cold as the meat will get hot during grinding.)

Using a large mincing dye, grind the brisket and short rib, along with the pork fat and any reserved beef fat.

Add the chuck steak to the mix, then go down a dye size and begin to mince. Keeping all the strands of meat in the same direction, stack them on top of each other, in a strand about 30 cm (12 inches) long. Wrap in plastic wrap, then gently push together to bind.

Now rest the meat in the fridge for a couple of hours.

Cut the meat into generous 3 cm (1¼ inch) slices. Fry in the rendered beef fat over medium-high heat for 2 minutes on each side to get a crust – you don't want the meat completely cooked through.

Rest in a warm oven for a couple of minutes.

Top with caramelised onions and cheddar. Slap in a bun and top with sauce, commit and eat.

AWESOME SECRET TIP

The yeasted doughnut recipe from page 27 makes a fabulous burger bun if you glaze it with a lightly beaten egg, sprinkle with sesame seeds and bake it in a hot oven for 10 minutes.

"This is definitely a commitment burger!"

"Be warned, the mix gets more volatile with time, and can serve some rough justice to family pests or rude customers alike."

WHY do we make fizz? It's what you have with burgers! As a child, I would run to the secret cave and dig out all manner of fizzers, to be deliberately shaken so the contents would explode all over Mum and Dad's unsuspecting guests at the dinner table. While we are still having trouble getting the bubbles to go downwards rather than upwards, and this concoction is pink not green, it's a quiet nod to Roald Dahl and his whimsical Willy Wonka creations.

MAKES ABOUT 7 LITRES (245 FL OZ/28 CUPS)

RHUBARB & PASSIONFRUIT FROBSCOTTLE

1 kg (2 lb 4 oz) rhubarb
2 lemons (preferably Meyer)
8 passionfruit
6 litres (210 fl oz/24 cups) water
450 g (1 lb) caster (superfine) sugar
50 ml (1½ fl oz) white vinegar

Wash the rhubarb, lemons and passionfruit, then thinly slice all the fruit. Place in a sterilised non-reactive bucket with the remaining ingredients. Stir until the sugar dissolves.

Cover with some muslin (cheesecloth) and leave at room temperature for 24–48 hours.

Remove the cloth from the top of the bucket and use it to strain the liquid from the solids. Toss out the solids.

Decant the liquid into sterilised plastic bottles, leaving about 2.5 cm (1 inch) clear at the top of the neck. Screw the lids on and store in a dark place for 2 weeks.

After 2 weeks, place the bottles in the fridge to slow the fermentation, otherwise your linen closet or pantry could come to a sticky end.

This fizz will last about 1 month, if you haven't inhaled it before then. It's that good!

GLOSSARY

acetate non-stick plastic sheets, used for lining moulds for easy release; available from craft shops and specialist cookware suppliers.

airbrush small, air-operated tool that sprays liquid in a fine mist.

ball tool an essential cake-decorating tool, used for modelling sugar paste and thinning the edges of moulded shapes.

cake leveller a frame with a height-adjustable wire, used to cut cakes into even, level layers.

cake ring a metal ring used to bake or set a cake in.

cake smoother flat, smooth, rectangular piece of plastic with a handle, used to smooth the surface of sugar paste to remove any bumps or indents.

citric acid white powder, stocked in the baking section of supermarkets, used to add an acidic or sour taste to foods and drinks.

CMC gum carboxymethyl cellulose, a harmless chemical added to sugar paste to form a strong modelling paste that dries hard. Can also be mixed with a little water to make a thick, strong, edible glue.

couverture chocolate high-quality chocolate containing extra cocoa butter that gives the chocolate more sheen, a firmer 'snap' when broken, and a creamy, mellow flavour.

cubeb pepper a pepper grown mostly in Sumatra and Java. It has a mild pepper flavour, with a hint of allspice.

cream of tartar tartaric acid, available from the baking section of supermarkets. It stabilises beaten egg whites, helps baked goods rise, and gives candies a creamier texture.

dextrose monohydrate a fine, white, highly soluble powdered sugar, with a delicate sweetness and great clarity, used in confectionery and ice creams.

dowels long, sturdy wooden or plastic sticks that can be cut to the required size, and used to support tiers in large cakes.

Dutch-processed cocoa powder has a deeper, darker colour and smoother flavour than regular cocoa powder, as it has been treated to neutralise its acidity. It is more expensive, but richer in flavour.

egg white powder dehydrated egg whites, which add stability to beaten egg whites. Sold in cake decorating stores and some health food shops.

florist's oasis dome a dome-shaped piece of foam with a rounded top and flat bottom, used by florists and cake decorators, to hold fresh flower arrangements in place and to keep them fresh.

florist's wire thin, flexible wire that can be cut to desired lengths, used to anchor flowers in position on cakes.

flower paste a ready-to-use paste containing edible gum, that can be rolled incredibly thin, making it ideal for moulding flowers for cake decorations. It is also known as gum paste or petal paste.

foam discs polystyrene discs used to support and separate tiers in large cakes.

gelatine a natural setting agent, available as a powder or thin, clear, flat sheets. We generally use gelatine sheets as they create a more transparent jelly than powdered gelatine, with a more neutral taste. One tablespoon of powdered gelatine is equivalent to about four sheets.

lace moulds silicon moulds used to imprint an intricate lace pattern onto sugar paste.

liquid malt a sweet, thick, malt-flavoured syrup, available from home-brew shops; also called malt extract.

modelling paste used in cake decorating, this is similar to flower paste, but less stretchy.

pandan paste a ready-to-use paste, made from the sweet, fragrant leaves of the tropical South-East Asian pandan tree. You'll find it at most Asian food stores.

pastry flour a low-protein flour, often used in pastry and other baking applications where a very tender finished product is desired. It is much softer and more finely textured than regular flour.

pearl string pearl beads fused on a string roll that can be cut to the desired length; used for decorative purposes.

pectin jaune a fruit pectin, added to jams and jellies to help them set. Available from speciality food stores.

scriber tool modelling tool, used to lightly score or mark patterns onto cakes, and for bursting air bubbles in icing.

shimmer dust a shiny, edible powder used in cake decorating to add sparkles of colour; also known as luster dust.

silicon baking mat a non-stick, flexible silicon mat used in baking; also useful in candy making, as it dissipates heat rapidly.

soft-ball stage refers to a specific temperature range (118–121°C/245–250°F) when cooking with sugar syrup; so named because the syrup will form a soft ball when dropped in cold water.

soft fondant a creamy confection, used as a filling or coating for cakes, candies and pastries.

sriracha sauce a multi-purpose hot Thai chilli sauce that is deliciously addictive. Widely available from Asian food stores.

strong flour used for making bread, and also known as bread flour or '00' flour. It has a higher gluten content than regular flour, so it becomes more elastic with heavy kneading, trapping air bubbles that help the dough rise.

sugar glue an edible glue used in cake decorating. Can be purchased ready-made, or made by mixing CMC gum with a little water.

sugar paste (rolled fondant) a pliable icing that moulds around cakes to give a smooth, perfect finish. It is known by many names, such as ready-to-roll icing, regal ice, plastic icing, pettinice and satin ice. The chocolate and almond/marzipan sugar pastes used in the Cakeatorium chapter come ready-made.

LETTERS

INDEX

Page numbers in *italics* refer to photographs.

A

B

C

D

E

F

G

H

I

J

L

ACKNOWLEDGEMENTS

Firstly we need to say to our beautiful daughter Matilda (Tilley TuTu), this is for you. You inspire and give us the drive to do all these crazy, weird, wonderful things each day.

Corinne Roberts for believing in us, and allowing us to have our own weird voice. Miriam Steenhauer and Susanne Geppert for your fabulous design and vision. Katri Hilden for your patience, sitting in our kitchen to edit as we bustled about preparing. Katy Holder for all the recipe edits and Katie Bosher for pulling everything together to make our book awesome.

Chris Crerar, the magic man with the camera — what can we say, you ROCK. Charlotte Bell for all your stylish ways.

Teena would like to thank her wonderful parents and family for their support and encouragement, endless hours of babysitting and, when we lived next door, for getting the house warm before we got home on all those cold winter nights.

Enormous gratitude must be given to our fabulous staff. We have been lucky since day one, and without you there would be no shop. David Osborne (Super Dave), Briallen Frisken (Boobs), Katherine Darling (KJ), Claire Benham (Hot Pants), Isabel Casey (Jinglebells), Matthew Trull (Mr Moo), Tim Calabria (Cupcake), Amber Lester (Twinkle Toes), Elizabeth O'Rourke (Betty Boop), Jessica Evans (Jess), GG, sidewinder, mad eye, not funny funny girl, the hyperventilator and the carpark bandit.

Thanks to Dave Boyer, Retro Phil with Scott and Vicky from Warwick Street Antiques, Chris Wisbey and Sally Dakis, Kelly Cloake and the Alabama Hotel, Rupert Bell, Jemima Wagner and Gus Mckay and his beautiful girl Serene for all the props and locations.

Lastly the good people who ended up captured in the book: Jo Crack, Zola Blackwood Coyle, Ned Fitzgerald, Leo Adams, Meg Bignell, Otto Bell, Bruno Bell, Luke Burgess, Dale Campisi, Teisha and Aaron Archer, Nat Gee, Amy Ko, Peri, Sofia and Ines Chislett, Rodney, Tristan and Chloe Dunn, Severine Demanet, Aedan Howlett, Ushi and Rolph Luetke-Steinhorst, Nick Cracknell and Mem, Memily just not Emily Rynne.

And thanks to all the punters who crave that endless sugar high!

Published in 2014 by Murdoch Books, an imprint of Allen & Unwin

Murdoch Books Australia
83 Alexander Street
Crows Nest NSW 2065
Phone: +61 (0) 2 8425 0100
Fax: +61 (0) 2 9906 2218
www.murdochbooks.com.au
info@murdochbooks.com.au

Murdoch Books UK
Erico House, 6th Floor
93–99 Upper Richmond Road
Putney, London SW15 2TG
Phone: +44 (0) 20 8785 5995
www.murdochbooks.co.uk
info@murdochbooks.co.uk

For Corporate Orders & Custom Publishing contact Noel Hammond, National Business Development Manager, Murdoch Books Australia

Publisher: Corinne Roberts
Design concept & illustrations: Miriam Steenhauer
Designer: Susanne Geppert
Photographer: Chris Crerar
Stylist: Charlotte Bell
Food editor: Katy Holder
Editor: Katri Hilden
Editorial managers: Livia Caiazzo & Katie Bosher
Production: Mary Bjelobrk

A cataloguing-in-publication entry is available from the catalogue of the National Library of Australia at www.nla.gov.au.

ISBN 978 1 74336 072 9 Australia
ISBN 978 1 74336 104 7 UK

A catalogue record for this book is available from the British Library.

Colour reproduction by Splitting Image Colour Studio Pty Ltd, Clayton, Victoria
Printed by 1010 Printing International Limited, China

IMPORTANT: Those who might be at risk from the effects of salmonella poisoning (the elderly, pregnant women, young children and those suffering from immune deficiency diseases) should consult their doctor with any concerns about eating raw eggs.

OVEN GUIDE: You may find cooking times vary depending on the oven you are using. For fan-forced ovens, as a general rule, set the oven temperature to 20°C (35°F) lower than indicated in the recipe.

MEASURES GUIDE: We have used 20 ml (4 teaspoon) tablespoon measures. If you are using a 15 ml (3 teaspoon) tablespoon add an extra teaspoon of the ingredient for each tablespoon specified.